CW00661439

1921

NORTHERN
IRELAND
CENTENARY
HISTORICAL
PERSPECTIVES

2021

CRAIG. — "Now, we've got our Parliament, Ned, what are we to do next?"

CARSON. — "How should I know? I'm out of politics."

'Craig and Carson' (30 May 1921), the Shemus Cartoon Collection, PD 4309 TX 81.

NATIONAL LIBRARY OF IRELAND

1921

NORTHERN IRELAND
CENTENARY
HISTORICAL
PERSPECTIVES

2021

EDITED BY

Caoimhe Nic Dháibhéid
Marie Coleman
Paul Bew

 ULSTER HISTORICAL FOUNDATION

Contents

Section I

Partition and the origins of Northern Ireland

"IT'S A LITTLE SOUVENIR I
BOUGHT FROM DUBLIN DEAR."

Cartoon by Rowel Friers (*c.* 1966).
Courtesy of Yvonne Friers.
Thanks also to Declan Martin, *Irish Politics in Postcards* (2016)

Section II
A century of Northern Irish life

General view of Coalisland, County Tyrone (*c*. 1900), L_CAB_08922.
NATIONAL LIBRARY OF IRELAND
Thanks also to Sammy McKay and Keith Beattie, *Light of Other Days Around Coalisland* (2021)

Poster for a Gaelic football match, Lurgan,
County Armagh, (1 Apr. 1923).

Ireland versus Scotland rugby
match (1922).

Notes on contributors

SÍOBHRA AIKEN is a lecturer in Irish at the School of Arts, English and Languages, Queen's University Belfast. Her publications include *The men will talk to me: Ernie O'Malley's interviews with the Northern Divisions* (2018), *An chuid eile díom féin: aistí le Máirtín Ó Direáin* (2018). Her monograph, *Spiritual wounds: trauma, testimony and the Irish Civil War*, will be published in early 2022.

BRIAN BARTON is a member of the Northern Ireland Centenary Historical Advisory Panel. He has authored or edited over a dozen books on Irish history and politics, including *The Belfast Blitz: the city in the war years* (2015), *The secret court martial records of the Easter Rising* (2010) and (co-authored with Michael Foy) *The Easter Rising* (2011). He also contributed chapters on Northern Ireland to *A new history of Ireland, vol. vii: Ireland, 1921–1984* (2003).

PAUL BEW is emeritus professor of politics at Queen's University Belfast and an independent cross-bench peer in the House of Lords. He chairs the Northern Ireland Centenary Historical Advisory Panel. His recent publications include *Churchill and Ireland* (2016) and *Ireland: the politics of enmity, 1789–2006* (2007). He has written biographies of John Redmond, Seán Lemass and Charles Stewart Parnell.

GRAHAM BROWNLOW is senior lecturer in economics at Queen's Management School. Since 2012 he has been an editor of *Irish Economic and Social History*. His historical research has involved topics as wide and varied as the rise and fall of linen, Home Rule, partition, rent-seeking and DeLorean. He has also written on the history and method of economics, covering Irish figures like T.K. Whitaker and George O'Brien as well as international figures such as Nobel laureate Douglass North.

MARIE COLEMAN is professor in twentieth century Irish history at Queen's University Belfast and is member of the Northern Ireland Centenary Historical Advisory Panel. Her publications include *The Irish Revolution,*

1916–1923 (2002), *County Longford and the Irish Revolution, 1910– 1923* (2001) and a number of academic articles on gender, religion and pensions during and after the Irish Revolution.

NIAMH GALLAGHER is a lecturer in modern British and Irish history and a fellow of St Catharine's College at the University of Cambridge. She is a member of the Northern Ireland Centenary Historical Advisory Panel. Her first book, *Ireland and the Great War: a social and political history* (2019), won the Royal Historical Society's Whitfield Book Prize in 2020.

ALISON GARDEN is a UK Research and Innovation Future Leaders fellow at Queen's University Belfast. She is the author of *The literary afterlives of Roger Casement, 1899–2016* (2020) and is working on her second monograph, a cultural history of 'love across the divide' during the Northern Ireland conflict.

ADRIAN GRANT is a historian and lecturer in politics at Ulster University. He is the author of *Derry: the Irish Revolution, 1912–23* (2018) and *Irish socialist republicanism, 1909–36* (2012). More recently his research has centred on urban history, with a focus on the impacts of housing regeneration on people and communities after the Second World War. Much of this work has also taken Derry City as a case study, exploring the varied impacts of physical changes to the city that occurred in tandem with the early years of the Troubles.

ANDREW R. HOLMES is reader in history at Queen's University Belfast. He has published extensively on the history of Protestantism and evangelicalism, including *The Irish Presbyterian mind: conservative theology, evangelical experience, and modern criticism, 1830–1930* (2018). With Gladys Ganiel, he is currently editing *The Oxford handbook of religion in modern Ireland*.

TOM HULME is a senior lecturer in modern British history at Queen's University Belfast. He is currently working on the history of male same-sex relationships in Belfast and has written on this topic for both *Gay Times* and *Irish Historical Studies*. His publications include *After the shock city: urban culture and the making of modern citizenship* (2019) and, edited with Professor Simon Gunn, *New approaches to governance and rule in urban Europe since 1500* (2020).

PETER LEARY is vice-chancellor's fellow in history at Oxford Brookes University. He is the author of *Unapproved routes: histories of the Irish border, c. 1922–72* (2016) and winner of the American Conference for Irish Studies Donald Murphy Prize. His articles on the history of the Irish border have appeared in various publications including *History Workshop Journal, Folklore* and the *Guardian*.

IAN MCBRIDE is the Foster professor of Irish history at the University of Oxford. His books include *Eighteenth-century Ireland: the Isle of Slaves* (2007), *Scripture politics: Ulster Presbyterians and Irish radicalism in the late eighteenth century* (1998) and *The Siege of Derry in Ulster Protestant mythology* (1997). He has recently completed work on *Irish political writings I*, a volume for *The Cambridge edition of the works of Jonathan Swift*. His current project is a book on Irish Catholics under the Penal Laws, based largely on archival sources in Rome.

LEANNE MCCORMICK is senior lecturer in modern Irish social history at Ulster University. She is the author of *Regulating sexuality: women in twentieth-century Northern Ireland* (2009) and co-author of the *Mother and Baby Homes and Magdalene Laundries in Northern Ireland, 1922–1990: report* (2021).

TIMOTHY G. MCMAHON is associate professor of history at Marquette University in Milwaukee, Wisconsin, and a past president of the American Conference for Irish Studies. He is the author of *Grand opportunity: the Gaelic Revival and Irish society, 1893–1910* (2008), editor of *Pádraig Ó Fathaigh's War of Independence: recollections of a Galway Gaelic Leaguer* (2000) and co-editor of *Ireland in an imperial world: citizenship, opportunism, and subversion* (2017).

GARETH MULVENNA is a Belfast-based researcher and author with a special focus on the history and culture of militant loyalism. His first book, *Tartan Gangs and paramilitaries: the loyalist backlash* (2016), was described by journalist Ed Moloney as 'a classic'. In 2020 he collaborated with Councillor Billy Hutchinson on the autobiography of his life in the UVF and Progressive Unionist Party, *My life in loyalism*.

CAOIMHE NIC DHÁIBHÉID is senior lecturer in modern history at the University of Sheffield and a member of the Northern Ireland Centenary Historical Advisory Panel. She is the author of two books, *Terrorist histories: individuals and political violence since the 19th century* (2016) and *Seán MacBride: a republican life, 1904–46* (2011). She is currently working on the history of emotions during the Irish revolutionary period.

MARGARET O'CALLAGHAN is a historian and political analyst at Queen's University Belfast and a member of the Northern Ireland Centenary Historical Advisory Panel. Her publications include *British high politics and a nationalist Ireland: criminality, land and the law under Forster and Balfour* (1994) and (co-edited with Mary E. Daly) *1916 in 1966: commemorating the Easter Rising* (2007). She is currently writing on partition and on Alice Stopford Green.

CONNAL PARR is senior lecturer in history at Northumbria University. His first book, *Inventing the myth: political passions and the Ulster Protestant imagination* (2017), was shortlisted for the Christopher Ewart-Biggs Memorial Prize and the Royal Historical Society's Whitfield Prize for distinguished first books. He is a board member of Etcetera Theatre Company and is currently completing his second book on the Irish Anti-Apartheid Movement.

HENRY PATTERSON is emeritus professor of Irish politics at Ulster University and is a member of the Northern Ireland Centenary Historical Advisory Panel. His publications include *Ireland's violent frontier: the border and Anglo-Irish relations during the Troubles* (2013), *Unionism and Orangeism since 1945: the decline of the loyal family* (2007), *The politics of illusion: republicanism and socialism in modern Ireland* (1989), *Ireland since 1939* (2006), *Class conflict and sectarianism: the Protestant working class and the Belfast labour movement 1868–1920* (1980) and *The state in Northern Ireland 1921–72: political forces and social classes* (1979). He is currently working on a history of unionism and class in post-war Northern Ireland.

RICHARD ROSE was professor of politics at the University of Strathclyde from 1966 until 2005. A fuller account of his experience conducting field research in Northern Ireland is in the chapter 'Northern Ireland: nothing civil about civil war' in *Learning about politics in time and space* (2014). He has written extensively on British politics and the Northern Ireland Troubles. He is director of the Centre for the Study of Public Policy, which he founded at Strathclyde, and researches as a visiting fellow at the European University Institute Florence and the Wissenschaftszentrum Berlin.

MARGARET SCULL is a historian of modern Britain and Ireland. Her first book was *The Catholic Church and the Northern Ireland Troubles, 1968–1998* (2019) and her current project examines the role of funerals and grief throughout the Troubles.

DAVID TORRANCE is the Northern Ireland specialist at the House of Commons Library. His most recent book is *'Standing up for Scotland': nationalist unionism and Scottish party politics, 1884–2014* (2020). Like all good Scots, he lives and works in London.

GRAHAM WALKER is emeritus professor of political history at Queen's University Belfast and a member of the Northern Ireland Centenary Historical Advisory Panel. Among his books are *The Labour Party in Scotland: religion, the union, and the Irish dimension* (2016), *A history of the Ulster Unionist Party: protest, pragmatism, pessimism* (2004) and *The politics of frustration: Harry Midgely and the failure of Labour in Northern Ireland* (1985).

TIM WILSON directs the Handa Centre for the Study of Terrorism and Political Violence at St Andrews University. He is the author of both *Killing strangers: how political violence became modern* (2020) and *Frontiers of violence: conflict and identity in Ulster and Upper Silesia, 1918–1922* (2010).

PRONI, CAB/3/G/13/4

General George C. Marshall inspecting US troops at a camp ceremony in Northern Ireland (Apr. 1942).

Abbreviations

CEDAW	Convention on Elimination of All Forms of Discrimination Against Women
CCA	Cork County Archives
DUP	Democratic Unionist Party
DHAC	Derry Housing Action Committee
DHSS	Department of Health and Social Security
FPA	Family Planning Association
INLA	Irish National Liberation Army
IPP	Irish Parliamentary Party
IRA	Irish Republican Army
IVF	Irish Volunteer Force
LGBT	lesbian, gay, bisexual and transgender
MAI	Military Archives of Ireland
MSPC	Military Service Pensions Collection
NAI	National Archives of Ireland
NHS	National Health Service
NIFPA	Northern Ireland Family Planning Association
NIGRA	Northern Ireland Gay Rights Association
NILP	Northern Ireland Labour Party
PD	People's Democracy
PSNI	Police Service of Northern Ireland
PRONI	Public Record Office of Northern Ireland
RIC	Royal Irish Constabulary
RUC	Royal Ulster Constabulary
SDLP	Social Democratic and Labour Party
TNA	The National Archives of the United Kingdom
UDA	Ulster Defence Association
UPAA	Ulster Pregnancy Advisory Association
USC	Ulster Special Constabulary
UUC	Ulster Unionist Council
UULA	Ulster Unionist Labour Association
UVF	Ulster Volunteer Force
UWC	Ulster Workers' Council
UUP	Ulster Unionist Party

'Trees in the wind' (*c.* 2019) by Clement McAleer.

Courtesy of the artist. This painting appeared in 'A New Tradition' in the exhibition *Portrait of Northern Ireland: neither an elegy nor a manifesto* (2021)

Introduction

CAOIMHE NIC DHÁIBHÉID, MARIE COLEMAN AND PAUL BEW

This book arises from the work of the Centenary Historical Advisory Panel established by the secretary of state for Northern Ireland in August 2020. The aim of the panel is to ensure that the history of Northern Ireland is understood in all its complexity, acknowledging that there are divergent views on the past. Our work has been informed by the *Principles of Remembering* produced by the Community Relations Council:

1 Start from the historical facts;
2 Recognise the implications and consequences of what happened;
3 Understand that different perceptions and interpretations exist;
4 Show how events and activities can deepen understanding of the period.
5 All to be seen in the context of an 'inclusive and accepting society'.[1]

As members of the Centenary Advisory Panel, the editors have brought together 20 essays from a range of scholars working on different aspects of the history of Northern Ireland since its foundation in 1921. This book does not claim to be a definitive history of Northern Ireland over the last hundred years. Rather, our aim is to explore a number of themes around its foundation and subsequent development. Some brush strokes are broader than others, but the book aims to give readers a sense of the diversity and vibrancy of scholarship on Northern Irish history in the twenty-first century.

The book is divided into two sections. The first examines in detail events surrounding the partition of Ireland, the foundation of Northern Ireland and the outworkings of the Boundary Commission established under the terms

'The Shadow' (1957) by E. Rutherford.
Courtesy of The Police Museum, Belfast and the artist's family.
This painting appeared in the 'Chronicling Conflict' section of the exhibition *Portrait of Northern Ireland: neither an elegy nor a manifesto* (2021)

of the Anglo-Irish Treaty of 1921. Niamh Gallagher sets the scene, exploring the transformed geopolitical context after the Great War, as empires retreated and the ideal of self-determination spread. The 'Irish question' or even the 'Ulster question' was not *sui generis*; rather, it was part of a broader global trend of decolonisation and democratic self-determination. Of course, the challenge for policymakers for Ireland north and south was to reconcile rival claims to self-determination from Irish nationalists and Ulster unionists. These claims were not made purely rhetorically; by 1920, increasing violence was darkening the political landscape. Paul Bew explores the different styles of the two great leaders of rival political communities in what would become Northern Ireland, James Craig and Joseph Devlin, emphasising the contradictions in their political journeys and underscoring that both were less absolutist than we might have thought. A number of authors trace the devastating effects of intercommunal violence in different parts of what would become Northern Ireland. Adrian Grant explores the dynamics of conflict in Derry/Londonderry which, in 1920/21, as in the 1880s and the 1960s, preceded the outbreak of serious violence in Belfast. Tim Wilson traces conflict in Belfast itself between 1920 and 1922, when that city was the deadliest part of Ireland and when intercommunal violence there reached unprecedented heights. The spillover effect was significant and, as Henry Patterson shows in a detailed account, deadly sectarian violence in Bangor in July 1920 was directly shaped by riots in Belfast earlier that month. The impact of this sectarian violence, which followed on the strains of the Great War, was felt across society, as Síobhra Aiken explores. The preponderance of treatments and regimes for 'nervous patients' in Northern Ireland in the 1920s suggests a society that was aware it had undergone great trauma, even if political divisions remained firmly entrenched.

The violence in Northern Ireland between 1920 and 1922 unfolded, of course, against the backdrop of renewed political uncertainty generated by negotiations for the Anglo-Irish Treaty of December 1921 and the Boundary Commission, which opened the possibility that the existing border around the six counties of Northern Ireland would be redrawn. Brian Barton introduces us to the relatively unknown figure of Diarmaid Fawsitt, who, as envoy of Dáil Éireann to Belfast in the winter of 1921/2, provides us with an eyewitness account of the political, economic and security situation there, albeit from a southern republican perspective. The Anglo-Irish Treaty threw the survival of Northern Ireland as a devolved part of the United Kingdom into question and, as David Torrance shows, unionist leaders were anxious to avoid any possibility that Northern Ireland could be co-opted, even momentarily, into the jurisdiction of the new Free State. As such, Northern Ireland did not secede from the Free State: it had never been part of it. Nevertheless, the Boundary Commission and the border continued to focus minds for much of the early 1920s. The presumed impending adjustment of the border created a number of flashpoints in 1922 and 1923: Margaret O'Callaghan excavates one such, showing how the Belleek–Pettigo incident of June 1922, when B-Special policemen launched an incursion into County Donegal (Free State territory), created ripples in London and in Dublin, and helps to illuminate the increasing pace of the drift to civil war south of the border. Timothy G. McMahon provides an expert overview of the workings of the Boundary Commission, including its never-implemented recommendations for transfer of territory, emphasising the ultimately successful political strategy adopted by James Craig in his 'not an inch' position. The border, of course, did not disappear with the suppression of the Boundary Commission report, and Peter Leary's chapter demonstrates how border communities continued to live with and across that line on the map through outbreaks of cross-border violence, attempts to disrupt cross-border traffic and the complexities of differing customs regimes.

The second section of book explores different aspects of Northern Irish life in the hundred years since its foundation. Graham Walker charts the innovations of devolution as it was implemented in Northern Ireland – which, from 1921 to 1972, was the only portion of the United Kingdom to enjoy (or endure) self-government. As Walker shows, the Northern Irish government frequently extracted significant political and financial concessions from Westminster, winning successive arguments about the importance of 'step-by-step' alignment with the rest of the UK. In this way, the possibilities and limits of devolution were carved out in practice by Stormont governments as they went along. Political identities continued and still continue to matter greatly in Northern Ireland, of course, and the great communal divides were deepened by the outbreak of the conflict commonly known as the Troubles in 1969. Richard Rose provides an eyewitness retrospective account of Northern Irish society on the eve of the Troubles, as the civil-rights movement was met by and fractured into devastating political and sectarian violence. Connal Parr traces the fortunes of left-leaning working-class unionism, from independent unionists in the early years of Northern Ireland to the Northern Ireland Labour Party (NILP) in the post-war period and the intersections between labour militancy and paramilitarism in the Ulster Workers' Council (UWC) strike of 1974. Margaret Scull traces the history of republicanism in Northern Ireland, focusing particularly on the period of the Troubles and emphasising the varieties of republicanism that sometimes violently coexisted in what was a diverse ideological movement.

Nevertheless, there is more to the history of Northern Ireland than the history of political violence and divided communities. A series of essays presents alternative lenses for exploring that history. Graham Brownlow analyses the economy of Northern Ireland in the post-war period, when the old heavy industries went into terminal decline but efforts to definitively restructure the economy proved unsuccessful. Brownlow suggests that simplistic explanations for the unevenness of Northern Ireland's economic performance, pointing either to political or non-political factors, cannot capture a highly interconnected reality. The social and cultural history of Northern Ireland is also explored by a number of scholars. Andrew R. Holmes examines the religious history of Northern Ireland over the past hundred years, emphasising common experiences despite doctrinal differences, particularly in shaping associational culture and leisure activities, in responding to the challenges of modernisation and post-war demographic growth and in the combination of a regional and global religious identity.

The history of young people in Northern Ireland is the subject of Gareth Mulvenna's chapter, which explores the rise of the teenager and associated youth culture. Music is a particularly important part of the story here, from the Teddy Boys' love of rock 'n' roll to the arrival of punk in the midst of the Troubles and rave culture in the 1990s. One aspect of the rich literary culture of Northern Ireland is explored by Alison Garden in her analysis of 'love-across-the-barricades' literature; the Kevin and Sadie books by Joan Lingard, with which many will be familiar, are the best-known examples. Tom Hulme examines the history of the lesbian, gay, bisexual and transgender (LGBT) community in Northern Ireland, from the continuing criminalisation of homosexuality until Jeff Dudgeon's courageous case in the European Court of Human Rights in 1981 to the legalisation of same-sex marriage in 2020. Despite this long history of formal political discrimination, as Hulme shows, there was a vibrant parallel gay culture in Northern Ireland and, by the 1970s, increasing campaigns for political rights for gay and lesbian people. Campaigns for social justice have also long been a feature of the women's movement in Northern Ireland, as Leanne McCormick shows. Controlling women's bodies has been a cornerstone of the patriarchal nature of Northern

'Abstract' (*c.* 1960)
by Alice Berger-Hammerschlag.

Courtesy of David Lennon Art. This
painting appeared in the 'Encounters'
section of the exhibition *Portrait of
Northern Ireland: neither an elegy nor
a manifesto* (2021)

Irish society and feminists of all political hues battled throughout the century
to liberalise access to contraception, to dismantle the architecture of
containment in the mother and baby homes that were found on both sides
of the communal divide, and to ensure free, safe and legal access to abortion
services for Northern Irish women in Northern Ireland itself.

With such a range of topics, themes and methodologies, there is no master-
narrative to be found in this book. Nor do we want to suggest one. Northern
Ireland has meant different things to different people in the century since its
foundation and ballast for multiple interpretations can be found in this
collection. This is partly why the history, literature and culture of Northern
Ireland remain such a vibrant topic for scholarship and creativity. We hope
this book will give readers a sample of that diversity.

---

[1] Community Relations Council, *Principles for Remembering* (Belfast, 2021).

Section I
Partition and the origins of Northern Ireland

Farming on Mahee Island (*c.* 1940s).
THE TURTLE FAMILY

KEY

(1) Alsace-Lorraine, ceded by France to Germany in 1871. Now to be returned.

(2) German-Austria: German speaking provinces of Austria.

(3) Czecho-Slovak, including Bohemia, Moravia, Silesia, and the Slovak people of Austria-Hungary, created a new (state) Republic, 1918.

(4) Poland, 1772: the first partition land acquired by Russia, Prussia and Austria-Hungary, to be a new Republic 1918.

(5) Finland was annexed by Russia 1809, declared their independence 1918.

(6) Ukraine: The last Ukraine state fell into the hands of Russia in 1775, created a new Republic in 1918.

(7) Hungary: After the division of Austria-Hungary by the independent nationalities 1918.

(8) Jugo-Slovak Commonwealth including Carniola, Croatia, Slavonia, Bosnia, Herzegovinia and Dalmatia occupied by German-Austria-Hungary 1879 and annexed by them 1908. Recognized as an independent nation 1918.

(9) Serbia was recognized by Treaty of Berlin 1878: Independence proclaimed a kingdom 1882.

(10) Montenegro: absolute independence acknowledged by Treaty of Berlin 1878, in the defeat of Ottoman Empire.

(11) Armenia divided between Turkey and Russia 1828, to be liberated and protected by the league of nations 1918.

(12) Dardanelles—A free passage to all ships and commerce of all Nations.

(13) Roumania—Boundary by Nationality.

Railroads ———————

Battle Lines — — — — —

Reordering the world in the aftermath of the First World War

NIAMH GALLAGHER

For centuries empires were the dominant mode of geopolitical organisation. Nation states gradually became more prominent following the French Revolution in 1789 and the 1848 revolutions and this shift accelerated after the First World War.

Maps which had previously coloured many parts of the globe pink – a colour traditionally associated with the British Empire but also used by the Portuguese and French empires – gradually became more colourful as new states sprang up (and then sometimes disappeared) in the transfers of power that marked the twentieth century. Yet the transition from empires to nation states was not a linear process. It was fragmented, violent and a constant tug-of-war between the old international order and what emerged as the new one. It took until the end of the Second World War for decolonisation to become unstoppable. In 1920, when Northern Ireland was created, no one – including political leaders, civil servants, radicals, Dublin Castle, and least of all the public – could have predicted how the world map might look a handful of years later, let alone a hundred years since then. The region was established in a moment of great global uncertainty.

'Peace Map of Europe' (1918) by Rand McNally & Co.

It is easy to see the partition of Ireland as an exclusive product of developments within the United Kingdom polity. There are long histories of conquest, rebellion and religious and political strife, disputes over citizenship and nationhood that seem entirely peculiar to the Anglo-Irish relationship. Partition was already in the minds of those statesmen who pondered what to do about the so-called 'Irish question' – the descriptor given by successive generations of officials to Irish problems, as if they were organic in nature and nothing to do with London – during the third Home Rule crisis. In some ways, the Government of Ireland Act 1920, which formalised partition, seemed like the inevitable result of a longer process.[1]

Yet the partition of Ireland was born of its moment, just as partitions in India, Palestine, Cyprus and later Bosnia and Kosovo were also products of their times. During and in the aftermath of the First World War a profound reconfiguration of power relations swept across large parts of the world, which had implications for Ireland, the UK and the British Empire. On the one hand, the British world system seemed to be at its zenith in 1919 and 1920, having survived four and a half tumultuous years that had brought down other empires. It had even expanded its territory, gaining mandates as spoils of war following the defeat of the Austrian, German and Ottoman empires – imperial entities which, like the Romanovs, vanished in the Great War's aftermath. On the other hand, it had never been so vulnerable, as the delicate balance of power that had helped to make British predominance possible in the nineteenth century was dramatically ruptured. The solution to the Irish question in December 1920 was responsive to these new realities.

Robert Gerwarth and Erez Manela have reminded us that the First World War did not end in 1918 for most of its participants and that longer cycles of violence convulsed much of the globe until at least 1923. In the French Empire, unrest reverberated throughout Algeria, Syria, Indo-China and Morocco, while in the east, Japan gained significant control over former Chinese territories and was challenged by nationalist revolt in Korea. In the Middle East and Asia Minor, additional ethnic, national and religious dynamics overlapped in complex ways in violent conflicts, many of which continue to plague the region. In the former Ottoman territories, genocide and ethnic cleansing were some of the earliest examples of horrors that would be replayed elsewhere throughout the century.

New blueprints for how to order the world gained traction during the inter-war period. The clash between Bolshevism and counter-revolutionary movements formed the backdrop of conflicts that stretched from 'Finland

and the Baltic States through Russia and Ukraine, Poland, Austria, Hungary, Germany, all the way through the Balkans into Anatolia, the Caucasus, and the Middle East, and even Czechoslovakia'.[2] Fascism, an alternative blueprint, gained rapid popularity and adapted to national contexts in Italy, Germany, Britain, Ireland and elsewhere. A new superpower, the United States of America, emerged on the international scene from 1917, moving epicentres of influence across the Atlantic and further upsetting the balance of power in Europe.

The British Empire – a system that contained an extraordinary range of shifting constitutional, political, diplomatic, commercial and cultural relationships – was far from immune to these developments. Unrest, which varied in scale and temperament and which predated the First World War in places, was rife in Egypt, India, Iraq, Afghanistan, Burma and, of course, Ireland. As in the other regions which were under imperial control or influence, or which had recently been part of an empire, power struggles were not a simple matter of indigenous colonised peoples protesting against their imperial overlords. They involved complicated overlapping dynamics. Nonetheless, anti-imperialism was a common refrain within discourses expressed by groups agitating against empire. From 1918 a new language of self-determination was in vogue following the speeches made by the American president, Woodrow Wilson, wherein he critiqued the European system and spoke in favour of the civil right of self-government. Self-determination became the key takeaway point for activists justifying their actions against the *ancien régime*. As Art O'Brien, president of the Sinn Féin Association of Great Britain, remarked after Terence MacSwiney's death from hunger strike:

> From the Atlantic to the Indian Ocean it is the same combat against the same enemy. Today, we're the avant-garde. But it isn't just for Ireland that the Lord Mayor has died, it is so that the whole British empire is destroyed.[3]

The newly created League of Nations, the first experiment in internationalism set up following the Paris Peace Conference in 1919–20, was petitioned by Irish and other nationalists who hoped that it might deliver self-government in their favour. Yet Wilson rapidly became uneasy with the League – as did the United States Senate, which voted against America joining it in November 1919 – and Manela has shown how anticolonial movements overinterpreted Wilson's covenant on self-determination. In many ways the

League was a counter-revolutionary institution designed to blunt the effects of the Bolshevik Revolution and recast self-determination in the service of empire.[4] Put simply, it did not want to tamper with existing borders. For black Atlantic leaders and intellectuals, it was also bound up with the politics of race.[5] Nationalists and anticolonial activists came up against the realisation that empires did not want to concede power and the League was not going to force their hand. For Irish nationalists, Ireland's claim to nationhood was seen by the League as a British matter to resolve. It took them some time to realise this, however, and from 1919 they put their energies into their own revolutionary activity as well as focusing on the international arena to achieve independence from the British system.

Conversely, many thinkers across the United Kingdom pondered solutions that would satisfy Irish unionists, particularly those in Ulster, as well as Irish nationalists, whilst keeping all of Ireland within the Empire. Imperial federation was an idea advanced by Alfred Milner and his network of civil servants, who had helped to manage post-war reconstruction in South Africa following the Second Boer War (1899–1901). Milner took up an important role in the British war cabinet, as minister without portfolio, from 1916, when David Lloyd George became prime minister, and continued to push for a federated empire to solve Ireland's difficulty and strengthen the Empire in a rapidly changing global context. Lloyd George was less keen on it, though for a time championed the stripped-down version – Home Rule all round.

The scheme also drew support from the Milnerites, Winston Churchill and others, and envisaged an early form of devolution across the United Kingdom, including parliaments for Scotland, Wales and Ireland (though debate existed over whether Ireland should have two parliaments and whether England, as the dominant partner, should have a parliament beyond the imperial seat at Westminster). Other suggestions were proposed by a wider range of groups right up until December 1920. In July, the Trades Union Congress passed a resolution demanding a single parliament for Ireland with full dominion status – which effectively happened the following year, but only for the 26 counties. The British Labour Party called for an all-Ireland assembly elected by proportional representation, while the faction of Liberals who had stayed with the former prime minister, Herbert Asquith, following the change of government in December 1916, demanded a referendum of sorts – an option for counties to choose whether they wished to be part of an Irish parliament.[6]

All of these solutions proposed to keep Ireland in the Empire, which seems to have been a central concern for those who deliberated in cabinet during 1920 and 1921. The resulting settlements – the Government of Ireland Act 1920 and the Anglo-Irish Treaty (1921) – both achieved that aim. Part of the perceived necessity to retain all of Ireland was the threat posed by an imagined scenario – if Ireland achieved self-government, a domino effect would happen across imperial territories. Such a fear was sufficient to split the Liberal Party in 1886 and reinvigorated the Conservative Party from the 1880s onwards as part of its strategy of reinvention under the banner of Tory democracy. Like Banquo's ghost, the domino-effect idea reappeared after the First World War at a time when challenges to British power were very real.

Nationalist unrest across the British Empire was only one part of a greater problem. The world economy had been blown apart as a result of the War, badly impacting British finances. In 1919 the economist John Maynard Keynes calculated that Britain would have to pay back its American loans at the rate of £100 million per annum, the equivalent of the annual revenue of India – an empire within the Empire – in 1917. Over one million Indians had served the British Empire during the war, accounting for the single greatest manpower contribution throughout the British world system. In the final years of war, India's resources were being pressed more and more heavily by the UK, and in 1917 the viceroy lent India's entire annual revenue to the UK – naturally, without the people's consent. The emerging Home Rule and non-cooperation movements under Annie Besant and Mohandas K. (Mahatma) Gandhi were a cause for concern.

Relations with the so-called White Dominions – where large British and Irish populations had settled in waves of emigration in earlier decades – were also not without friction. Over a million men from the Dominions had served in the war. Eighteen per cent of ANZACs (members of the Australian and New Zealand Army Corps) were British- and Irish-born emigrants; the figure is higher again for the Canadians. For those who served overseas the proportion of those killed was shockingly high: 14 per cent of New Zealanders, 15 per cent of Canadians and almost 19 per cent of Australians.[7] Challenges ranging from problems within the City of London (the Empire's financial centre), trade-union strikes (tanks were sent to Glasgow in January 1919 to curb labour strife), the loss of private commerce, expenditure on the army and navy to manage the unruly Empire, and a rising superpower across the Atlantic that was itself a republic and contained many citizens sympathetic to the Irish republican demand for independence, were all part of the contexts in which the six-county solution appeared as the final scheme out of a range of options debated up until the final hour in 1920.[8]

The eventual solution arrived at was heavily influenced by these pressing challenges. The increasing popularity of Sinn Féin after the April 1918 conscription crisis and the War of Independence that followed would have been inconceivable without the context of the Great War. Unionist opposition and Conservative support were intimately bound up with empire, and in 1920 and 1921 the threats to the imperial order seemed all the more real. The revolutionary violence throughout Europe, north Africa and Asia Minor and the rise of Bolshevism (ironically, fascism was much less of a concern in the early 1920s) threatened to undo the status quo and build a new world order based on the working classes, most of whom in the UK had only gained the vote in 1918. Anti-socialism was part of the propaganda presented by the coalition government and new Conservative-led administration from 1920 until 1922 to tarnish trade unionists and build national unity around the notion of post-war stability.

The Ulster Unionist Party (UUP) employed the same technique, linking Bolshevism to Catholicism in its propaganda. This ensured that Northern Ireland's foundations remained secure amidst the War of Independence and prevented the working classes of the six counties from joining forces, as they were doing elsewhere in Europe, threatening the unity that had been built around the constitutional question.[9] Meanwhile, Irish nationalists continued to dream of an independent Ireland that could be achieved with international support in spite of the 1920 Act, though those dreams were tempered in 1921 and later, in 1925, when the report of the Boundary Commission was suppressed.

A solution for Ulster might have been on the horizon since 1914 but the final outcome was tied up with shifting contingencies. How different groups responded to the events between 1920 and 1925 was also linked to the opportunities and challenges presented by the reordering of the world system during and after the First World War. The war was the third major climacteric when politics in Ireland was transformed by international trends, the first being the seventeenth-century conquests and the second, the 1798 Rebellion and 1801 Union. And the legacies of those formative post-war years would haunt the island's twentieth century.[10]

FURTHER READING

Bourke, Richard and Niamh Gallagher (eds), 2022 *The political thought of the Irish Revolution*. Cambridge. Cambridge University Press.

Darwin, John, 2009 *The empire project: the rise and fall of the British world-system, 1830–1970*. Cambridge. Cambridge University Press.

Gerwarth, Robert and Erez Manela (eds), 2014 *Empires at war: 1911–1923*. Oxford. Oxford University Press.

Gettachew, Adom, 2019 *Worldmaking after empire: the rise and fall of self-determination*. Princeton. Princeton University Press.

Gingeras, Ryan, 2011 *Sorrowful shores: violence, ethnicity, and the end of the Ottoman Empire, 1912–1923*. Oxford. Oxford University Press.

Manela, Erez, 2007 *The Wilsonian moment: self-determination and the international origins of anticolonial nationalism*. Oxford. Oxford University Press.

Pedersen, Susan, 2015 *The guardians: the League of Nations and the crisis of empire*. Oxford. Oxford University Press.

NOTES

[1] Ronan Fanning, *Fatal path: British government and Irish revolution, 1910–1922* (London, 2013).

[2] Robert Gerwarth and Erez Manela (eds), *Empires at war: 1911–1923* (Oxford, 2014), 10.

[3] John Horne, 'Ireland at the crossroad, 1920–21: nation, empire, partition', Media Library Speeches, *President of Ireland*, 25 Feb. 2021, https://president.ie/en/media-library/speeches/ireland-at-the-crossroad-1920-21-nation-empire-partition (accessed 2 Aug. 2021).

[4] Erez Manela, *The Wilsonian moment: self-determination and the international origins of anticolonial nationalism* (Oxford, 2007); Susan Pedersen, *The guardians: the League of Nations and the crisis of empire* (Oxford, 2015).

[5] Adom Gettachew, *Worldmaking after empire: the rise and fall of self-determination* (Princeton, 2019).

[6] J.E. Kendle, 'The Round Table movement and "Home Rule All Round"', *Historical Journal*, vol. 11, no. 2 (1968), 332–53; Richard Murphy, 'Walter Long and the making of the Government of Ireland Act, 1919–20', *Irish Historical Studies*, vol. 25, no. 97 (May 1986), 82–96.

[7] The figures for Dominion participation overseas are 400,000 Canadians (60,000 deaths), 332,000 Australians (62,300 deaths) and 115,000 New Zealanders (16,000 deaths): War Office, *Statistics of the military effort of the British Empire during the Great War, 1914–1920* (London, 1922), 756–73. My thanks to John Horne for this reference.

[8] John Darwin, *The empire project: the rise and fall of the British world-system 1830–1970* (Cambridge, 2009).

[9] Alan Parkinson, *A difficult birth: the early years of Northern Ireland, 1920–25* (Dublin, 2020).

[10] I wish to thank John Horne for providing feedback on a draft of this article.

Sir James Craig (1870–1940).
PRONI, D2334/4/1/10

Two great communal leaders
Sir James Craig (1870–1940)
and Joe Devlin (1871–1934)

PAUL BEW

One hundred years ago the political leadership of the two communities in Northern Ireland effectively lay in the hands of two men, James Craig and Joe Devlin. They were very different: Craig was born into a wealthy family; Joe Devlin came from a poor working-class background. Both men made substantial reputations for themselves in Westminster. Both made tactical mistakes but neither man was petty.

Craig's early years in politics were dominated by the strength of the land-reform politics of T.W. Russell, which presented a serious challenge to the political ambitions of the Craig family. This formative experience left him throughout his career with a perhaps exaggerated fear of the willingness of Protestants to split on social issues and thereby weaken the unionist cause. In 1922, the senior British civil servant S.G. Tallents described Craig as having 'a great desire to do the right and important thing: not a clever man but one of sound judgement and can realise a big issue', but he also noted critically that ministers were 'too close to their followers' – a serious problem throughout the first five decades of devolution.[1] The physical threat from the Irish Republican Army (IRA) was substantial in 1921 but it diminished after the outbreak of the Irish Civil War in June 1922. Serious ideological pressure on the unionists remained, but in 1938 Whitehall mandarins were surprised to find that the Craig cabinet was still too close to its followers.

Alas, both Craig and Devlin at times employed the language of threat – Craig was more culpable here than Devlin. But, on the positive side, Craig always set his face against an explosive all-out sectarian civil war. He played a major role in the 'peace process' of 1921–2 by meeting Éamon de Valera in May 1921 before the truce in July – a physically brave act at a time of serious violence. In doing this, Craig put himself in the service of the peacemaking faction of the British state, a faction much distrusted by other unionists. Again in 1922, Craig twice negotiated pacts with Michael Collins. He faced down senior unionist critics, who hated this search for compromise with republican men of violence.

In 1921 Craig was capable of saying, 'The rights of the minority must be sacred to the majority ... it will be broad views and tolerant ideas that we here can make an ideal of the parliament and executive.' In 1926 he was capable of saying:

The North and South have got to live together as friendly neighbours: So it is for the government of the South and the government of the North to turn their hands rather from the matters which may have divided them in the past to concentrate on the matters which really affect the welfare of the people in their own area with a view that the whole of Ireland, and not one part of it alone, may be prosperous.[2]

Yet, in 1927, he announced the abolition of proportional representation, which understandably infuriated Joe Devlin.

Craig's actions here partly reflect his long-term, deeply neurotic fear of Protestant and unionist splits. In the 1930s, as ministers in Dublin happily talked of 'building a Catholic constitution for a Catholic state', he was happy to talk of 'a Protestant parliament for a Protestant people'. It was a far cry from his more liberal language in the 1920s, but it has to be recalled also that, when Carson wanted to carry on the war with the IRA in 1921, Craig was determined to take a major and ultimately successful risk for peace. Carson's hysterical maiden Lords' speech in 1922 blamed everyone but himself for the turmoil and anarchy in Ireland; this was simply not Craig's style.

The nationalist politician Joe Devlin is a figure of enormous complexity. When Parnell came to Belfast to give his conciliatory speech in May 1891, Devlin, a youthful anti-Parnellite in the split, attacked his carriage. Parnell's message was that Irish nationalism faced a fatal drag on its aspirations unless it conciliated the reasonable or unreasonable prejudices of the unionist community in the north-east. It was not a message the young Devlin was keen to hear. In the early 1900s Devlin was an opponent of the local Catholic bishop. In 1902 he became the MP for Kilkenny. He was the loyal and principal ally of John Dillon, alongside John Redmond, the key leader of the Irish Parliamentary Party (IPP) in this era. Devlin became the leading figure in the powerful Ancient Order of Hibernians, who helped many access the new Liberal welfare reforms after 1906.

Joe Devlin became the hero of Belfast's Catholic factory workers, especially the female linen workers. Henry Patterson's important essay on Bangor, elsewhere in this volume, shows how much Devlin contributed to improvements in their lives. On the other hand, critics like the Cork MP William O'Brien pointed out that the Ancient Order of Hibernians was a Catholic-only sectarian organisation – mirroring the Orange Order on the other side – which neither Parnell nor Tone could have joined. Devlin initially resisted any form of partition in the Home Rule crisis but in the end came to accept John Dillon's view of 1914 that it was wrong to coerce the unionists. He was never, however, a supporter of the Belfast parliament and his involvement after 1926 was either languid or sharply critical of the government.

Devlin criticised the unionists not just for their sectarianism but also for their social conservatism. In a speech in early 1921, 'He asked what bond of comradeship could he feel with men who in the past voted against such reforms as Old Age Pensions.'[3] He had applauded Winston Churchill's vision of Home Rule as expressed in Churchill's Belfast speech of February 1912 – in which Churchill promised that after Home Rule Irish old-age pensioners who draw a state pension 'as their last refuge on this side of the grave'[4] would continue to receive it. The irony here, of course, is that an independent Irish government in 1924 had to cut the level of pension support inherited from the United Kingdom, while in the north it was sustained. Devlin was not surprised. He was a lifelong opponent of Sinn Féin precisely because of his concerns on such a point.

Devlin's attractive and warm personality transcended politics. There was genuine unionist grief at the moment of his death. Hugh Pollock, the Ulster Unionist minister of finance, was an intimate personal friend. Sir Edward Herdman insisted that Devlin commanded large-scale unionist respect, while John Johnstone delivered what was styled the 'Omagh Unionist tribute': they

Courtesy of Declan Martin,
Irish Politics in Postcards (2016).

might not agree with his politics, but 'the country had sustained the loss of a generous charitable gentleman, who, according to his views, fought wholeheartedly in the best interests of his native land'.[5] The most interesting account came from the veteran *Northern Whig* writer E.T. Robinson:

> 'Our Joe' as old Northern Nationalists used affectionately to call him said many bitter things in the course of political word warfare but he never did a mean or unkind action ... Apart from politics, everybody who knew him liked Mr Devlin, and his quick sympathy with distress or trouble of any kind made him regarded with real affection by a large portion of the community.[6]

Joe Devlin was decidedly not a republican, but he was never impressed by the parliament of Northern Ireland, not even after his decision to drop abstention in 1926. But the fact remains that he was always an important presence in Belfast, as he was in Westminster. James Craig's importance is acknowledged in a physical sense in the Stormont central hall. Lord Carson, never having sat in Stormont, was acknowledged there in a statue, even though he, like Devlin, was unenthusiastic about devolution in Northern Ireland. Is it not time to mark also the role of Joe Devlin by some physical monument? At this centenary moment, it is time to challenge the fact that he was the one truly great actor of 1921 who is not properly acknowledged in the building of our parliament.

FURTHER READING

Bew, Paul, Gibbon, Peter and Patterson, Henry, 2002 *Northern Ireland 1921–2001: political forces and social classes*. London. Serif.
Hepburn, A.C., 2008 *Catholic Belfast and nationalist Ireland in the era of Joe Devlin, 1871–1934*. Oxford. Oxford University Press.
Mulvagh, Conor, 2016 *The Irish Parliamentary Party at Westminster, 1900–18*. Manchester. Manchester University Press.

NOTES

[1] Paul Bew, Peter Gibbon and Henry Patterson, *Northern Ireland 1921–2001: political forces and social classes* (London, 2002), 26.
[2] Ibid., 5.
[3] *Yorkshire Post*, 21 Feb. 1921.
[4] Paul Bew, *Churchill and Ireland* (Oxford, 2016), 57.
[5] *Derry Journal*, 22 Jan. 1934.
[6] *Northern Whig*, 19 Jan. 1934.

Anticipating partition in Derry

ADRIAN GRANT

The city of Derry was no stranger to sectarian violence prior to 1920. As in Belfast, industrialisation stimulated a rise in the Catholic population during the nineteenth century.

The image of Derry, or Londonderry, had been distinctly bound up with Protestantism, and later unionism, since the plantation of Ulster in the early seventeenth century. The construction of the defensive walled city of Londonderry during the years between 1613 and 1619 provided an eponymous and sustained actual link to the English capital, while the cultural memory of the siege of Derry (1688–9) clearly delineated the 'walled city' as a Protestant and unionist space. However, Catholics formed a majority by 1851 and soon thereafter began more forcefully to express the politics of Irish nationalism in public space. Tensions rose in the late 1860s, resulting in ongoing sectarian violence between 1868 and 1870 and flaring into a major riot in 1869. Further serious rioting took place in 1883 and was attributed to escalating disputes over the use of public buildings and space within the walls by nationalist political groups.

These peaks in sectarian violence represent the rising intensity of contestation over the spaces of the city and the identity of the city itself. The fruitless partition proposals of 1912 allowed the seeds of anxious discontent to germinate in the minds of both nationalists and unionists until 1914 and beyond. The gravity of the situation in Derry became apparent as the frequency and seriousness of riots increased. A growing militancy was accompanied by a spike in sales of revolvers in 1913, after which guns became more common during altercations. The Royal Irish Constabulary (RIC) shot a bystander dead in one such riot on 14 August 1913.[1] His death was the first as a result of political violence in the period between 1912 and 1923.

The Twelfth of August (1919).

While the wider constitutional questions of the day drove the politics and violence of the period, questions over the future status of Derry city gave tensions a sharper edge than those occurring elsewhere. Captain Jack White, who served as commander of the Irish Volunteer Force (IVF) in Derry during 1914, thought the city was the place most likely to spark the kind of violence that could advance to a wider civil conflict. Volunteers under his command believed the Ulster Volunteer Force (UVF) was planning to invade and occupy the city and even staged a mock battle on a Donegal beach in anticipation of this. [2]

Sectarian tensions reached a high point between March and August 1914, during which time the Larne gun-running took place, and the IPP accepted the county option as a concession to unionism. Under this proposed scheme, the counties of Ulster would hold plebiscites to determine whether their inhabitants wished to come under the jurisdiction of the Home Rule parliament in Dublin or to remain under the jurisdiction of Westminster. The nationalist leadership in the north-west made this concession, comfortable in the knowledge that Derry city would be afforded county status for such a purpose and would almost certainly opt to come under the Dublin parliament along with Donegal, Fermanagh and Tyrone. County Londonderry would likely remain under Westminster, but there was little consternation about such a prospect in the nationalist city, which tended to gravitate west rather than east. The county-option proposals collapsed following unionist opposition and there was now a real fear, for both unionists and nationalists, that in the event of partition Derry could go either way. The physical expression of this tension abated almost overnight on the outbreak of the war in Europe. The uncertain prospect of partition continued to haunt the city throughout the war and after.

While the abortive partition proposals of 1916 very clearly included Derry city within the excluded six-county area, a nervous streak continued to run through the local unionist population. A six-county partition scheme would separate the city from neighbouring Donegal, which also had a sizable unionist population. This bitter pill eventually became palatable, at least to unionists within the six counties. Derry unionists were also consumed by a well-founded anxiety that the city's majority nationalist population possessed the necessary political clout to ensure that the city would fall under Dublin control, either in a united independent Ireland or as the result of a revised partition agreement. Sinn Féin's performance in the post-war general election of 1918 ensured that this nervousness was unabated going into 1919, when

IRA activity also began to increase throughout the country. A large-scale show of unity between nationalists and republicans in the city during a parade on 15 August 1919 provoked alarm for unionists. A crowd of 5,000, including IRA members and 1,000 demobilised soldiers in uniform, marched together around the city and through the gate in the walls at Bishop Street, where the banners of Sinn Féin and the IPP were symbolically entwined. Small-scale scuffles and fighting occurred at interface areas that night, representing a re-emergence of the kind of violence that had not been seen in the city since 1913 and 1914.[3]

This display of nationalist–republican unity was significant. The municipal elections due to take place in 1920 were the first to be held using the proportional-representation electoral system. Prior to this, unionists held control of local government and the mayoralty of the city, essentially in perpetuity, despite representing a minority since the mid-nineteenth century. This was achieved mainly through an electoral ward system that ensured unionist-majority areas returned a greater number of councillors than the overcrowded nationalist wards. Fearing the impact of proportional

LEFT TO RIGHT: Captain Jack White, Commander James McGlinchey, Colonel Maurice Moore, Celtic Park, Derry (1914).

IRISH INDEPENDENT

18

Barricade at the
Fountain, (1920).

representation on this delicately balanced structure, the unionist-controlled corporation further refined the boundaries in 1919 against vociferous charges of gerrymandering from nationalists. [4] Regardless, the impact of proportional representation transcended the ward revisions and resulted in the return of a nationalist/republican majority to Londonderry Corporation for the first time. The independent nationalist Hugh C. O'Doherty was elected mayor – the first Catholic to hold the post since 1688.

One of O'Doherty's first acts as mayor was to propose a ban on flags flying from the Guildhall. [5] This was ostensibly an act designed to allow all residents to identify with the council but, in reality, meant the removal of the union flag from the premier public building in the city. He also refused to attend official functions where a loyal toast was made. These actions were tempered, however, with O'Doherty's call for the incoming corporation to focus on major issues of social concern, including a housing shortage and problems with the water and electricity supplies. Meanwhile, the headline-grabbing actions of the Sinn Féin/IPP-controlled corporation continued to irk the unionist community. Sinn Féin, for instance, proposed a motion to have the lord lieutenant, Viscount French, removed as a freeman of the city after he advocated letting republican hunger strikers in Mountjoy Prison die. Plans were also put in place to revise the ward boundaries to reflect the population more proportionately, thereby increasing the likelihood that local government would remain under nationalist control. [6]

Consideration of the Government of Ireland Bill, which included provision for two separate bicameral parliaments for Northern Ireland and Southern Ireland respectively, did little to ease tensions in Derry. Most felt it probable that Derry would be included in the northern jurisdiction, but there was also a strong feeling that control of local government in the city, and places like Fermanagh and Tyrone, would be crucial to determining the shape of a lasting settlement. The Government of Ireland Act, after all, was ignored by most in the country, regardless of the fact that the Ulster Unionists enthusiastically used it to establish the institutions of Northern Ireland from 1921 onwards.

Derry seems to have been on an inevitable slide towards serious violence throughout the spring and early summer of 1920. Weekend riots grew increasingly serious until, on the night of Saturday, 19 June 1920, gunmen emerged from the Fountain area of the city and began firing towards a crowded city centre. IRA members returned fire in an attempt to force the attackers to retreat. The unionists took control of the Diamond and Bishop Street area and held it for a number of hours, even after the arrival of soldiers from the Dorset Regiment, who were stationed in the city. Two people, uninvolved in the fighting, were killed. The IRA took over St Columb's College as a headquarters and were joined by a large contingent of armed and trained nationalist ex-servicemen. This pan-nationalist front was reinforced with machine guns and ammunition shipped from Redmondite contacts in Donegal, stoking unionist fears of an invasion of the city from the south.

The violence spiralled further out of control during the course of the following week and, by the time martial law was finally imposed on 24 June, 20 people had died and a huge number had been injured. The *Irish Independent* called it 'war, pure and simple', while an IRA participant said that Derry was like 'a town on the Western Front'. The events of the week went beyond the usually uncontrolled rioting, with sectarian targeting and killing occurring on both sides. The *Derry Journal* and many nationalists alleged collusion between the police, the army and the unionist vigilantes. These charges were denied in official circles, but evidence certainly exists to warrant such suspicions.[7]

Thereafter, a large police force, a reinforced military contingent, curfew orders, the securitisation of the city and the existence of a formidable loyal population combined to ensure significant IRA activities in Derry were rare, with the exception of a few sporadic actions prior to the truce in July 1921. While the violence receded, the motivating factor of partition remained top of the local political agenda. The ceremonial opening of the Northern Ireland parliament in Belfast on 22 June 1921 provided Derry unionists with an increased confidence that, despite nationalist control of local government, the trajectory of political events was in their favour. However, the Anglo-Irish Treaty signed on 6 December 1921 provided for the appointment of the Boundary Commission to decide on the final position of the border between Northern Ireland and the soon-to-be-established Irish Free State. As the political debate over the treaty dominated Irish politics throughout the early part of 1922, Derry nationalists felt confident that they could make a strong case for the city to be included within the jurisdiction of the Free State. [8] Control of Londonderry Corporation was central to this strategy, which was spearheaded by the mayor with support from nationalists and pro-treaty republicans. The Free State government buttressed this confidence through, for example, the payment of northern nationalist teachers' salaries in an attempt to undermine the legitimacy of Northern Ireland. [9] Clandestine plans were drawn up for a joint IRA force to invade the north in spring 1922 and ineffective attempts had already been made to provoke a northern 'rising'.[10] When civil war broke out in the south on 28 June, however, focus shifted from the border to the internal strife that such a conflict entails.

The Civil War ended in 1923 and the Boundary Commission was belatedly initiated in 1924. By this time, the unionist position in Derry had been significantly strengthened. One of the earliest acts of the Northern Ireland

Bishop's Gate, Derry (1920). *The Illustrated London News*

EMPLOYED WITH A LEWIS GUN TO DISPERSE SNIPERS : AN ARMOURED CAR AT BISHOP'S GATE, DERRY, DURING THE DISTURBANCES.

government, in 1922, was to abolish proportional representation in local elections. The following year, the nationalist majority lost control of Londonderry Corporation and along with it went the propaganda potential and actual resources that were envisaged as essential tools to make a strong case for Derry to be ceded to the Free State. Ultimately, the Boundary Commission recommended the transfer of part of east Donegal to Northern Ireland rather than the transfer of Derry into the Free State, as was expected by nationalists and feared by unionists. The 1920 border was maintained and the Boundary Commission report shelved as part of a political and financial agreement between the British, Northern Ireland and Free State governments. The anticipation of partition, which had been a negative experience for nationalists and unionists since 1912, finally evaporated with the Boundary Commission debacle in 1925. Even as the people of the wider area actually experienced partition – with customs checks, border posts and the reality of diverging political entities seeping into everyday life – there remained widespread apprehension around Derry's eventual constitutional reality on the partitioned island of Ireland. The unionist position prevailed, but the sustainability of a largely manufactured minority control of the local-government apparatus would be continually called into question during the following decades. By 1968, the confluence of international and local events under the banner of civil rights would test that sustainability up to and beyond breaking point.

FURTHER READING

Fox, Colm, 1997 *The making of a minority: political developments in Derry and the north, 1912–25*. Derry. Guildhall Press.

Grant, Adrian, 2018 *Derry: the Irish Revolution, 1912–23*. Dublin. Four Courts Press.

Keohane, Leo, 2014 *Captain Jack White: imperialism, anarchism, and the Irish Citizen Army*. Kildare. Merrion Press.

Lynch, Robert, 2006 'Donegal and the joint-IRA northern offensive, May–November 1922', *Irish Historical Studies*, vol. 35, no. 138, 184–99.

Phoenix, Eamon, 1994 *Northern nationalism: nationalist politics, partition, and the Catholic minority in Northern Ireland, 1890–1940*. Belfast. Ulster Historical Foundation.

NOTES

[1] Illegal importation and distribution of arms, and reports of seizures of arms, 1911–14 (The National Archives of the United Kingdom (TNA), Colonial Office, 904/28); *Londonderry Sentinel*, 16 Aug. 1913.

[2] Leo Keohane, *Captain Jack White: imperialism, anarchism, and the Irish Citizen Army* (Kildare, 2014), 160–5; *Donegal Independent*, 4 July 1914.

[3] Adrian Grant, *Derry: the Irish Revolution, 1912–23* (Dublin, 2018), 48, 50, 92–3.

[4] *Derry Journal*, 29 Aug. 1919.

[5] Colm Fox, *The making of a minority: political developments in Derry and the north, 1912–25* (Londonderry, 1997), 69, 71.

[6] *Derry Journal*, 2 Feb. 1920; *Dublin Evening Telegraph*, 29 May 1920; Grant, *Derry*, 95.

[7] Grant, *Derry*, 98–102.

[8] *Derry Journal*, 11 Jan. 1922.

[9] Eamon Phoenix, *Northern nationalism: nationalist politics, partition, and the Catholic minority in Northern Ireland, 1890–1940* (Belfast, 1994), 157.

[10] Robert Lynch, 'Donegal and the joint-IRA northern offensive, May–November 1922', *Irish Historical Studies*, vol. 35, no. 138 (Nov. 2006), 189.

Infamous attacks on women

Sectarian violence in Bangor in July 1920

HENRY PATTERSON

A week after the outbreak of serious sectarian violence in Belfast in July 1920, Joe Devlin, the nationalist MP for West Belfast, raised the issue in the House of Commons. Although he focused on the devastating and murderous violence in Belfast, he also denounced attacks on Catholics that had been carried out in the seaside resort of Bangor. He produced angry denials from unionist MPs when he claimed that Bangor was the only town in Ireland where there had been 'infamous attacks on women'.[1]

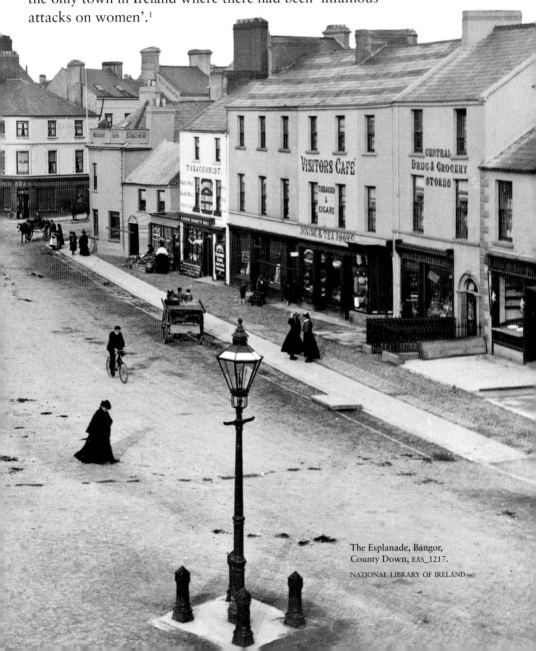

The Esplanade, Bangor,
County Down, EAS_1217.

The disturbances in the town had not resulted in deaths or serious injuries but had involved the attempted burning down of a hostel where over a hundred Catholic mill workers were enjoying a holiday break, as well as attacks on Catholic-owned hotels, pubs and shops. Soon suppressed in local memory, the outbreak of sectarianism and the reaction of the town's Protestant and unionist elite to these incidents is illustrative of the longer-term challenge for unionism of controlling plebeian loyalist violence.

Twelve miles from Belfast and connected to the city by rail since 1865, by the end of the century Bangor was being promoted in Britain and the south of Ireland as the Brighton of the north. In the mid-nineteenth century, Belfast factory owners and merchants had begun to build villas on the headlands and bays along the north-Down coast. They were joined by an expanding middle class and increasing numbers of skilled and supervisory workers as the town became a dormitory for Belfast. The population doubled to 8,300 between 1891 and 1911 and numbered over 13,000 by 1920. Cheap weekend return rail and steamer tickets brought the working class of Belfast in their droves during the months of July and August and there were also regular steamers from Scotland and the north of England, with the result that the town's population could more than double at the height of the season.[2]

Its modern origins lay in the area's colonisation by the Scottish landowner Sir James Hamilton in the first decade of the seventeenth century. Initially a predominantly Presbyterian town, by the time of partition there was also a substantial Church of Ireland community. Catholics represented eight per cent of the town's population.[3] Bangor Catholics worshipped in St Comgall's, which had been built on the south-western edge of the town at the end of the 1880s. Those walking to the church from the town centre would cross the Belfast railway line using the provocatively named Boyne Bridge. At some distance from the town centre, it was not a target for the mob in 1920.

Although north Down had been a centre of support for the United Irishmen in 1798, by the end of the nineteenth century it was firmly unionist and Orange. Bangor's Protestant population had mirrored the broader pan-class unionist alliance during the Home Rule crisis. They were led by four local gentry families: the Sharman Crawfords; the Dufferin and Avas; the Clanmorris/Wards; and the Perceval-Maxwells. These were joined by Belfast industrialists like Sir Samuel Davidson, the founder of the Sirocco engineering works in east Belfast, whose mansion, Seacourt, overlooked Bangor Bay. In April 1914, the north-Down UVF blockaded the town to allow the unloading of 4,000 Mauser rifles from the SS *Clyde Valley*. Many in the UVF volunteered to fight during the First World War, including Davidson's eldest son, who died on the first day of the battle of the Somme.[4] Prosperous, securely Protestant and unionist, the town had had little forewarning of trouble.

Joe Devlin was particularly concerned about the arson attack. He had helped to raise £10,000 to convert the Grand Hotel on the seafront into a hostel to provide holidays for female linen workers.[5] He had opened the hostel in April and he planned to spend the summer in the town, where he had rented a house. He claimed that on the previous Friday warnings had been given that the hotel would be burnt, and that in the early hours of Saturday petrol was poured over the woodwork, under which straw was placed and set on fire. A hundred or so women and girls had to flee the building. The fire brigade, police and volunteers succeeded in extinguishing the fire and, later on Saturday, a detachment of soldiers was sent to guard the hotel over the remainder of the weekend.[6]

The military presence did not prevent a further outbreak of violence on the Saturday evening. The town had been thronged with holidaymakers when a group attacked a young man, alleging that he was a 'Sinn Feiner'. To save him, the police put him in a motor car that belonged to the chairman of the urban council, a prominent unionist and Orangeman. The crowd then proceeded to attack the car, breaking the windscreen, lamps and hood and forcing the police to remove the victim, who was bruised and shaken, to the barracks. What the *Belfast News Letter* described as 'the hooligan crowd' then armed themselves with stones from the beach and proceeded upon a systematic tour of the town centre, breaking the windows and in some cases looting the contents of hotels and businesses owned by Catholics.[7]

The next day there was an emergency meeting of local magistrates and councillors called by the chairman, Thomas Wilson, whose car had been wrecked the previous evening. A shipowner and shipping agent, Wilson was also an active worker for the unionist cause, a member of the Standing Committee of the Ulster Unionist Council (UUC) and honorary secretary of the North Down Unionist Association.[8] He had been an officer in the UVF at the time of the gun-running episode.[9]

Wilson complained that 'the fair name of Bangor had been besmirched ... by an apparently organised crowd of rowdies. Valuable property had been destroyed, several shops had been looted, and people had been terrified.' He proposed that civilian patrols be formed to cooperate with the police and asked 'responsible people' in the town 'to exercise moral suasion and assist in maintaining order in the event of any further ebullition'.[10] He had come from a meeting with local Orangemen who had volunteered to take their share in patrolling the town. Wilson had also met with General Hackett-Pain, the divisional police commissioner for the north of Ireland who, he claimed, approved of the setting up of civilian patrols. The patrols would wear white armlets but would not be armed, and a member of the RIC would accompany each picket.

Wilson and other speakers at the meeting did not mention the fact that the crowd had targeted only Catholic properties. However, the only Catholic councillor, J.E. Kelly, broke the silence on the issue by describing what had happened as a sectarian riot. He added that, although he was far from blaming the ordinary citizens of Bangor, he had heard from the police that there were some local men involved. He was alone in dissenting from the proposal to set up civilian patrols, saying that sufficient troops should be sent to protect lives and property in the town.

When the patrols began to function the next night about half of them were composed of local Orangemen. In the main Protestant churches that Sunday

Children's Corner, Bangor, County Down, L_CAB_06008.

there was strong condemnation of Saturday's events. Reverend J.A. Carey of Bangor Parish said he could speak for his congregation in 'deploring such conduct, especially the wrecking and looting of the property of innocent and inoffensive people'. He pointed out that the authorities did not attribute the work to 'any respectable portion' of the Protestant population in Bangor. They were justly proud of Bangor and the good order and conduct and spirit of cooperation of all classes'.[11] Wrecking and looting could only bring discredit on the town and place a burden on the rate-payers.

An article in the *Freeman's Journal* suggested a possible cause of the Bangor violence in the fact that it was practically a suburb of Belfast and that a large percentage of the inhabitants were shipyard workers.[12] This was an exaggeration, as only the highest-paid workers could afford to rent a house in Bangor and travel daily to Belfast. Bangor's working class was small and mostly worked in building, transport and distribution. Those shipyard workers who lived in the town were from the skilled, technical and supervisory occupations. As in the rest of the UK, these were part of the labour aristocracy, with strongly ingrained notions of respectability and no time for the lumpen excesses of 'rowdies' and 'hooligans'.

The *Freeman's* emphasis on the role of shipyard workers may have reflected the presence at the Bangor meeting of the local councillor, Alex McKay. McKay, a shipyard worker himself, was a prominent member of the Ulster Unionist Labour Association (UULA) and had spoken at the mass loyalist meeting that had precipitated the shipyard expulsions the week before. The UULA had been propagating the idea that during the war Belfast and other Ulster towns had been 'invaded' by Catholics, who took the jobs of Protestants who had enlisted. These Catholics now represented, it was feared, a republican fifth column. On the day of the disturbances Bangor's local paper demanded to know 'What is the North Down Unionist Association doing to counteract if they cannot prevent this invasion of anti-Britishers?'[13]

McKay claimed that the working men of the town strongly deprecated what had taken place and would do all in their power to prevent any further trouble.[14] For labour unionists like McKay, the answer to the Sinn Féin threat was not mob violence but a state-sponsored militia, the armed special constabulary that Carson and Craig were pressing the British government to establish. At an entertainment for the Bangor B-Specials held in 1924 by the urban council, the chairman, now Sir Thomas Wilson, dated the effective formation of the Specials to the 1920 meeting that organised the civilian patrols: 'Not one bit of trouble had arisen since and Bangor was regarded as one of the most peaceful and best ordered towns in Northern Ireland.'[15]

The dilemma for unionist political leaders and the landed and industrial elite was to mobilise and control popular opposition to Sinn Féin and the IRA. Decades of experience demonstrated that political and military polarisation was likely to result in outbreaks of sectarian violence. The UVF and later the Ulster Special Constabulary (USC) or B-Specials were created, in part at least to discipline plebeian loyalist violence. Pearse Lalor in his study of sectarian outbreaks in Lisburn in 1920 supports this view: 'In east Belfast, as in Lisburn, the special constables were in fact created to control the wilder elements of rampaging loyalist mobs.'[16]

Bangor would not suffer from another outbreak of sectarian violence until the Troubles. The town soon recovered its reputation as a popular destination for tourists, including a considerable number from the Free State. The violence of July 1920 was forgotten about. In 1935, when two Belfast men were tried at the petty sessions for assaulting attendants at a local amusement park, District Inspector McKinley of the Royal Ulster Constabulary (RUC) expressed his desire to keep Bangor free from disorderly conduct:

> Bangorians are fortunate in living in a town where little of the rowdy element gets loose, even although our town is a mere twelve miles from the city of Belfast where undisciplined mobs undoubtedly exist.[17]

Eunan O'Halpin has noted an important historiographical gap in how anti-nationalist violence in Belfast and other towns in east Ulster was later recalled, explained and commemorated within loyalist communities.[18] Bangor suggests that at least for many middle-class unionists, sectarian violence, particularly against a defenceless minority, was something to be ashamed of and embarrassed by. One purpose of the creation of the B-Specials was to reserve the capacity to defend Northern Ireland to state forces and deny it to the mob. However, as Councillor Kelly's intervention demonstrated, Catholics would have preferred to be protected by the military – who, as O'Halpin points out, did not distinguish between contending groups of rioters and 'would fire impartially on crowds failing to disperse'.[19] The long-term problem for Northern Ireland was that this meant Catholics having to accept that the state's security would be protected by their Protestant neighbours.

FURTHER READING

Bew, Paul, Gibbon, Peter and Patterson, Henry, 2002 *Northern Ireland 1921–2001: political forces and social classes*. London. Serif.
Farrell, Michael, 1983 *Arming the Protestants: the formation of the Ulster Special Constabulary and the Royal Ulster Constabulary, 1920–7*. London. Pluto Press.
Hepburn, A.C., 2008 *Catholic Belfast and nationalist Ireland in the age of Joe Devlin, 1871–1934*. Oxford. Oxford University Press.
Lawlor, Pearse, 2009 *The burnings 1920*. Cork. Mercier Press.
Magill, Christopher, 2020 *Political conflict in east Ulster, 1920–22: revolution and reprisal*. Woodbridge. Boydell Press.
O'Halpin, Eunan and Ó Corráin, Daithí, 2020 *The dead of the Irish Revolution*. London and New Haven. Yale University Press.
Patterson, Henry, 1980 *Class conflict and sectarianism: the Protestant working class and the Belfast labour movement 1868–1920*. Belfast. Blackstaff Press.

NOTES

1 *Belfast News Letter*, 27 July 1920.
2 W.G. Lyttle, *The Bangor season* (Belfast, 1978), 32.
3 Government of Northern Ireland, *Census of Northern Ireland, 1926: County of Down* (Belfast, 1928), Table 18: Religious professions, 70.
4 Public Record Office of Northern Ireland (PRONI), Davidson family papers, D3642.
5 A.C. Hepburn, *Catholic Belfast and nationalist Ireland in the age of Joe Devlin, 1871–1934* (Oxford, 2008), 215–16.
6 *Belfast News Letter*, 27 July 1920.
7 *Belfast News Letter*, 26 July 1920.
8 *Belfast News Letter*, 17 Nov. 2020; Ian Wilson, 'Sir Thomas Wilson, pillar of Ulster society – and bootlegger!', *Bangor Historical Society*, 11 Apr. 2019, https://www.bangorhistoricalsocietyni.org/DATABASE/ARTICLES/articles/000027/002724.shtml (accessed 2 Aug. 2021).
9 Ian Wilson, *North Down: a century of photographs* (Bangor, 1999), 46.
10 *Belfast News Letter*, 27 July 1920.
11 Ibid.
12 *Freeman's Journal*, 26 July 1920.
13 *North Down Herald*, 24 July 1920.
14 *Belfast News Letter*, 27 July 1920.
15 *North Down Herald*, 8 Mar. 1924.
16 Pearse Lawlor, *The burnings 1920* (Cork, 2009), 98.
17 *Northern Herald*, 12 Oct. 1935.
18 Eunan O'Halpin and Daithí Ó Corráin, *The dead of the Irish Revolution* (London and New Haven, 2020), 19.
19 Ibid.

Rioting on York Street, Belfast (1 Sep. 1920).

Belfast Telegraph

The Belfast Troubles at one hundred

TIM WILSON

At the inauguration of the Northern Ireland parliament (22 June 1921) King George V delivered his famous plea for 'all Irishmen to stretch out the hand of forbearance and conciliation, to forgive and forget'.

In its immediately local context this was a decidedly optimistic invitation. Less than two weeks earlier the mutilated corpses of the police death squads had still been turning up on the hills that rise behind west Belfast. Less than three weeks later, a renewed cycle of intercommunal violence in the city was to take twenty-two lives.[1]

In all, perhaps 498 people lost their lives during the Belfast Troubles: 'a per capita death rate higher than that of any other part of the country between 1920 and 1922, including the legendary fighting areas of Munster, so famed in republican tradition'.[2] By early 1922 the killing rate in Belfast had hit its twentieth-century peak: 285 deaths in just six months. In 1972, the city's total fatalities were again to reach a similar magnitude (298), but this later killing was to be spread out over a full 12 months.[3] The 1920s Troubles reached a unique intensity.

The question is: why? Clearly, the macro-context must be a key part of any explanation. Unlike the post-1969 Troubles, this conflict was part of a much wider Irish revolution. The weak Belfast IRA – only 400 strong at its height – proved difficult to suppress, not least because of London's capricious and inconsistent delegation of local security policy to the emergent Northern Ireland government.[4] The USC was first established (from October 1920), then effectively suspended (from 11 July 1921) and then (after 22 November 1921) finally reestablished, reinforced and massively rearmed until there was one policeman for every six families in Northern Ireland. A force of no fewer than 10,000 Specials was projected for the Belfast area alone.[5]

The distinctive feature of the Belfast Troubles was their civilian character. As a result, Belfast's gunmen – and, crucially, their female supporters – often remain obstinately faceless to us. Major gaps remain in our understanding of 'freelance' Hibernian and loyalist violence in particular. [6] But an overall pattern is clear enough:

> Very few of the hundreds of IRA actions did not inspire some kind of reprisal activity from extremist elements in the loyalist population. It is a telling statistic that almost 75 percent of all people killed in Belfast died within a few days of a major IRA attack of some kind.[7]

What has been less explored is how sectarian violence itself was evolving. This was a period in which both the nature and quality of urban violence shifted profoundly during a relatively short period. Such processes deserve more analytical attention than they typically receive.

A first point to notice is how far the Great War had militarised the business of crowd control. Rioting was now routinely suppressed using automatic weaponry. Over that first troubled summer of 1920 the British military shot dead at least 38 civilians in Belfast. Seven were killed by a single burst from a Hotchkiss machine gun, discharged late on 29 August in the Marrowbone district. By international standards such killing remained relatively restrained. By local standards this was a new departure. No one had died in the 1912 riots.[8]

Such tactics help explain why the massive set-piece rioting of July and August 1920 was not repeated. Street disturbances did not disappear in Belfast, but they do seem to have become smaller. Photographs taken from an upper floor of the Grand Metropole Hotel on Thursday 2 September 1920 are useful here. The camera points down York Street, a major thoroughfare. A loyalist crowd – about 100 are in the frame – drives back a nationalist crowd using stones. Judging from the cloth caps, it seems to be a working-class crowd. Some have bicycles, suggesting reasonable wage-earning power.

One watching gentleman with walking stick and boater looks emphatically bourgeois: he may be a hotel guest. Body language and positioning – that is, how close together the members of the crowd are near the front – seems suggestive of a range of engagements ranging from enthusiastic participation to mild curiosity. No women seem to be present, although this may simply reflect a normal snapshot of city-centre life on a working day. No police or military are in sight on this occasion.

In general, though, the Belfast Troubles were profoundly shaped by security measures that were unprecedented for both their extent and duration. The city remained under continuous curfew from July 1920 to December 1924. In an age of traveller innocence, it was this general security presence that visitors first noticed: the unexpected luggage searches for arms on arrival; the sandbagged machine-gun posts incongruously planted amidst terraced rows of red-brick houses; and the armoured cars and lorries careering through the streets. If Belfast became 'an underworld … with deadly forces of its own' (to borrow Winston Churchill's phrase) then it was to some extent because a saturation security presence had submerged, and fragmented, its traditional massed confrontations.[9]

Change also came from below. Both the weapons and skills of trench warfare helped recast sectarian rioting into a very different type of conflict. Expectations shifted; as one police officer put it in early 1922: 'we thought stone-throwing was a terrible affair. I don't know what some of the old-time rioters would say if they could come back and see the "bhoys" of the present day with their rifles, grenades, and revolvers.'[10] Grenades and home-made bombs, it is worth noting, had been quite unknown before the First World War. By the early summer of 1921 they had emerged as a standard weapon of choice. A Catholic priest visiting east Belfast a few months later has left us this vivid (if highly jaundiced) vignette:

> Just at this moment a typically Belfast product passed, namely, a couple of working girls from the Newtownards Road. They were hatless, slatternly in dress, with pale, vicious faces and insolent eyes. At the lodge gate one said to the other: 'There's where they flung a bomb,' and both laughed.[11]

Brutalisation in the Belfast Troubles thus advanced through the relentless accumulation of such small-scale atrocities. It is striking that the overall proportion of female fatalities in the 1920s disturbances was about twice that of the post-1969 Troubles (15.88 per cent compared to 8.6 per cent).[12]

A mutual drift towards more indiscriminate targeting is unmistakable by early 1922. At first IRA volunteers had disdained sectarian rioting as a 'stone-throwing competition';[13] by November 1921 they were bombing shipyard trams. For their part, motorised B-Specials pioneered tactics of roving intimidation. Such drive-by shootings and bombings seem to have lacked the deliberate targeting characteristic of the loyalist travelling gunmen of 50 years later. But the hint of the future is clear enough, at least in retrospect.

There were limits. The UK was not one of the vanquished states after 1918. Indeed, in the final analysis, ceilings on escalation in Belfast were set in London by 'traditional assumptions that British rule stood for justice, righteousness and good laws'.[14] Thus the spectacular slaughter of six members of the McMahon family by a loyalist death squad (24 March 1922) directly prompted a major peace initiative led by Winston Churchill – the second Craig–Collins Pact (30 March 1922). London could react sharply enough when it wanted. Things were only allowed to fall apart so far.

Seen at a century's distance, though, the Belfast Troubles of 1920 to 1922 still stand out as a key formative phase in the city's evolution. The initial expulsions of Catholics (and socialist Protestants) from the shipyards, which began on 21 July 1920, did have a residual pogromic quality to them. This was largely traditional. Much the same, indeed, had happened in both 1886 and 1912. But within the wider Irish context, the Catholic minority in the city could afford some resistance, at least for a while and to some extent. Belfast was not Odessa.

What was genuinely new, however, was the severe elongation and fragmentation of more traditional conflict patterns. Security pressure from above, but also a grass-roots proliferation of guns and bombs, briefly combined to raise the spectre of a brand-new type of sectarian conflict. Its hallmark was its disproportionality. An armed few had shown how to create general mayhem. In May 1922 the city's very first peace wall was erected on the Newtownards Road; its successors stand there still.

FURTHER READING

Cunningham, Niall, 2013 'The social geography of violence during the Belfast Troubles, 1920–22', CRESC Working Paper No. 122. Manchester. Centre for Research on Socio-Cultural Change.

Farrell, Michael, 1983 *Arming the Protestants: the formation of the Ulster Special Constabulary and the Royal Ulster Constabulary, 1920–7*. London. Pluto Press.

Glennon, Kieran, 2013 *From pogrom to civil war: Tom Glennon and the Belfast IRA*. Cork. Mercier Press.

Lynch, Robert, 2006 *The northern IRA and the early years of partition 1920–1922.*
Dublin. Irish Academic Press.

McDermott, Jim, 2011 *Northern divisions: the Old IRA and the Belfast pogroms
1920–22.* Belfast. Beyond the Pale.

Magill, Christopher, 2020 *Political conflict in east Ulster, 1920–22: revolution and
reprisal.* Woodbridge. Boydell Press.

O'Halpin, Eunan and Ó Corráin, Daithí, 2020 *The dead of the Irish Revolution.*
London and New Haven. Yale University Press.

Wilson, T.K., 2010 '"The most terrible assassination that has yet stained the name of
Belfast": the McMahon Murders in context', *Irish Historical Studies*, vol. 37,
no. 145, 83–106.

NOTES

1   Eunan O'Halpin and Daithí Ó Corráin, *The dead of the Irish Revolution*
(London and New Haven, 2020), 514.

2   Robert Lynch, 'The people's protectors? The Irish Republican Army and the
"Belfast Pogrom," 1920–1922, *Journal of British Studies*, vol. 47, no. 2
(Apr. 2008), 375.

3   Kieran Glennon, *From pogrom to civil war: Tom Glennon and the Belfast IRA*
(Cork, 2013), 263; Niall Cunningham, 'The social geography of violence during
the Belfast Troubles, 1920–22', CRESC Working Paper No. 122 (Manchester,
2013), 3.

4   Robert Lynch, *The northern IRA and the early years of partition 1920–1922*
(Dublin, 2006); Jim McDermott, *Northern divisions: the Old IRA and the Belfast
pogroms 1920–22* (Belfast, 2001).

5   Michael Farrell, *Arming the Protestants: the formation of the Ulster Special
Constabulary and the Royal Ulster Constabulary, 1920–7* (London, 1983), 46.

6   Robert Lynch, 'The people's protectors? The Irish Republican Army and the
"Belfast Pogrom," 1920–1922', *Journal of British Studies*, vol. 47, no. 2
(Apr. 2008), 389; Christopher Magill, *Political conflict in east Ulster, 1920–22:
revolution and reprisal* (Woodbridge, 2020), 63.

7   Lynch, 'The people's protectors?', 389.

8   O'Halpin and Ó Corráin, *The dead of the Irish Revolution*, 151, 152–5, 159, 165,
168–70, 172, 175, 186; T.K. Wilson, '"The most terrible assassination that has yet
stained the name of Belfast": the McMahon murders in context', *Irish Historical
Studies*, vol. 37, no. 145 (May 2010), 89.

9   Cited in Eamon Phoenix, 'Political violence, diplomacy and the Catholic minority
in Northern Ireland, 1922' in John Darby, Nicholas Dodge and A.C. Hepburn
(eds), *Political violence: Ireland in a comparative perspective* (Ottawa, 1990), 35.

10   *Northern Whig*, 14 Feb. 1922.

11   P.J. Gannon, 'In the catacombs of Belfast', *Studies: An Irish Quarterly Review*,
vol. 11, no. 4 (June 1922), 281.

12   Cunningham, 'Social geography of violence', 7.

13   Lynch, 'The people's protectors?', 381.

14   D.G. Boyce, *Englishmen and Irish troubles: British public opinion and the making
of Irish policy 1918–22* (Cambridge, Massachusetts, 1972), 99.

The Dáil cabinet's mission to Belfast
1921–2

BRIAN BARTON

Julitta Clancy, an archivist, recalls being contacted by her Fawsitt cousins in March 2018. They had been inspecting the family farmhouse in west Cork following a storm and, on entering the loft, had discovered tea chests and suitcases brimming with documents concealed behind a partition wall. Julitta thought they might be the remaining papers of her late grandfather, Judge Diarmaid Fawsitt (1884–1967).

Over the next ten days she examined them. Remarkably, most were in good condition, though there was evidence of dampness and rodent and insect infestation. Sorted and filed, they filled 27 boxes.

Among the papers were Fawsitt's diaries, writings, speeches and legal briefs, and files germane to his work in the Industrial Development Association both in Cork and nationally. There was voluminous correspondence, much of it from the United States, where he had spent some time following his deportation from Cork in 1915, and had been Ireland's first consul general (1919–22). There were letters from Australia, where he had briefly emigrated in the early 1900s. There was one from Michael Collins referring to threats to his life; it was dated three days before his death at Béal na Bláth. But the most unexpected find was documents relating to Fawsitt's involvement in Northern Ireland affairs. Following the truce (11 July 1921) he had been recalled from his post in New York and initially appointed 'technical adviser' to Robert Barton, minister for economic affairs and one of five plenipotentiaries engaged in the treaty negotiations. Then, in November, the Dáil cabinet commissioned him to undertake a special mission – to Belfast. He was familiar with the city, having gone there promoting Irish industry several times before 1919.

Fawsitt visited Belfast five times between November 1921 and January 1922. The prescribed purpose of his mission was to ascertain the views of its businessmen regarding the fiscal 'guarantees' they thought 'necessary to foster and safeguard the [city's] industrial and commercial life'. He was to 'point out' to them how 'a single national authority within Ireland would serve the interests of [its] ... big business'. Those he interviewed, at least 16 in total, were mainly 'men representative of [its] ... economic life' and of the professions. Those he already knew provided him with 'letters of introduction' to others. Several were 'Protestant Home Rulers', but a number were prominent members of the UUC and the Orange Order. From the outset he made it clear to them that, though 'attached to' Barton's ministry, his visit was 'private and unofficial'. Their receptivity to his initiative encouraged him to stray beyond his original brief.

The timing of Fawsitt's first visit to Belfast (28 November 1921) was inauspicious: civil disorder had resulted in 27 fatalities between 19 and 25 November; Protestant paramilitary membership had soared to 21,000; an IRA campaign was gathering momentum; unemployment was mounting; and unionists were feeling betrayed by the terms of the truce and the pressure being applied to Craig, even by Conservatives, to accept all-Ireland institutions. In his subsequent report to Dublin (3 December 1921) Fawsitt set the scene: a curfew had just been imposed; there were 'lots of military in armoured cars' on the streets and 'shootings and bombings in the business heart'. Economic conditions were 'depressing': shipbuilding was reeling from the world surplus in tonnage, linen firms were 'stagnant', and the banks were in a 'delicate' condition. But, he stated, 'the prevailing obsession of businessmen' was the Irish boycott on goods from the north-east (it had been imposed following the expulsion of Catholic workers from the shipyards in July 1920). It was like 'a wall of steel', he said, and they spoke 'frankly of its crushing effects'. They regarded it as a 'stupid policy ... demonstrating absolutely the utter unfitness of the present Southern leaders to govern'. Fawsitt stated that 'these conditions ... obsessed [them] ... and influenced their outlook to a very marked degree'. There was, he observed, a 'double fear' – 'politicians live in constant fear of the mob', while manufacturers dreaded 'impending bankruptcy ... political and commercial ruin', and were 'beginning to consider ... the measures necessary to avert the calamities so feared'.

Fawsitt then discussed the 'political outlook'. He noted how Belfast's industrialists had always 'devotedly' supported 'political union' with Britain, 'the most powerful of modern empires', and also 'commercial union with upwards of 40 million of prosperous Britishers'. They believed that this 'lent a status and a stability to [their] … trade and commerce' which 'would be absent' were they 'in a small and weak state [Southern Ireland], independent of Britain', with an 'impoverished population of scarcely more than four million'. Fawsitt recognised that, up until 1914, they had 'prospered exceedingly'. But, he continued, 'war and its aftermath of unsettled … conditions' had 'disturbed' their 'economic mind' and 'occasioned a searching into the soundness of [this] … faith … The loss of British and overseas markets, the crushing impost of British taxation and the fickleness of political allies in G[reat] B[ritain] have impelled' them 'to a reconsideration' of their 'position'. He claimed that both they and their leaders in government 'recognise today' that 'home and foreign events will compel Belfast into political unity with all Ireland in the not remote future'. He regarded 'this tendency' as 'a valuable and powerful factor towards political settlement now'.

In support of these conjectures Fawsitt quoted, without attribution, a letter probably written by R.V. Williams, a local linen manufacturer, who was described by Alec Wilson (one of Fawsitt's other interviewees) as being 'well inside the ring of Ulster Unionist circles although not Orange or a Covenanter'. It stated that 'The Conservative Party has assassinated Ulster … There is no hope for us in English political alliance … We should be far safer negotiating with an avowed enemy [Sinn Féin]', than with a "false friend".' He continued: 'I believe Ulster is in a strong position … Sinn Fein [sic] is desperately anxious to win her over', and that 'Ulster would gain her ends much more easily and much more certainly by negotiating with [it] … direct'. He recognised that 'the great difficulty in the way' was the 'natural exasperation of Ulster caused by Sinn Fein tactics. The boycott is a horrible piece of stupidity … The Ulsterman is the last man on God's earth to be intimidated'; but, he added of Sinn Féin's leaders:

[If they] have any true sense of values they will see in Ulster's betrayal by English Tories … an opening for fraternal advances … What an effect might be caused … were the boycott to be called off, and a real and lasting truce to be proclaimed? … If Sinn Fein were to say to Ulster: 'we desire only brotherly relations … We acknowledge your rights and privileges and we do not wish to trespass on them; we desire but to reconcile them with our own … We withdraw the gunman … I believe a great many Unionists in Ulster think as I do today.

Fawsitt reported that all those he interviewed during his visit 'desired a political understanding' with the south. They had suggested that the 'best way to secure this was by means of a conference' of Ireland's national leaders but recognised that, because of the 'highly inflamed political atmosphere in Belfast', they would be 'reluctant to participate'. The businesspeople therefore favoured organising 'an informal chat between private citizens of influence on each side' that 'could prepare the way'. Fawsitt was convinced that his interviewees were 'sincerely desirous of winning a settlement', would 'press the acceptance of their views upon [their] ... political leaders' and were 'of sufficient weight ... to secure for whatever views they may advance a respectful and serious consideration'. In his opinion the industrial and commercial elite continued 'to carry most influence with Belfast civic and political leaders'.[1]

After the Anglo-Irish Treaty was signed (6 December 1921), Fawsitt received several letters that confirmed this optimistic analysis. One, from Alec Wilson, a Protestant Home Ruler, urged Sinn Féin immediately to make a 'gesture of real friendship' towards the north, as it 'would have a most marked effect upon men's minds hereabouts'. R.V. Williams wrote two of the other letters. In the first, he asserted:

> Things have changed since I saw you in Belfast ... I have been astonished to find, since the Treaty was published, how strong a feeling there is in the business community ... in favour of our accepting an Irish Parliament.

He confidently predicted: 'if the Dáil accepts the Treaty, Ulster will be ready to go into an Irish Parliament'. Though he anticipated 'strong opposition from the extreme element, the Orangemen' and others, he claimed that 'the majority' was 'in favour of coming to terms at once'. He also indicated that he was forming a 'businessman's committee, to influence our parliament in [this] ... direction'.[2]

Fawsitt received this letter on 13 December and returned to Belfast the next day. On arrival Williams handed him a second letter, which elaborated on the first. In it he asserted that 'Sinn Fein can go far towards winning Ulster by showing a conciliatory spirit.' Its people were 'suspicious' but, he said, they were 'in a mood to listen', and he listed the commitments they would require from Dublin. He appealed for Sinn Féin to make a 'declaration' that it 'is friendly and sympathetic' and 'desires to show the fullest consideration of Ulster's political aspirations'. Also, Belfast's industrialists would 'need to be assured that no tax whatever will be imposed on any raw materials used' in their manufactures, and 'that no attempt will be made to levy taxes on exports'.

In addition, the Protestant population would have to be satisfied that education would be free 'from any kind of clerical control' and that their schools would not be 'dominated by an educational policy which will be chiefly Roman Catholic'. He regarded 'the language question' as being of 'great importance' as well. He wrote: 'Ulster will require guarantees' that in those areas 'mainly English or Scotch in race, there will be no attempt to make the Irish language compulsory in the schools or that ignorance of [it] … will be a bar to promotion in the public services'; but he concluded:

> beyond these various points, and more important than them all, is the necessity for showing a genuine desire to adopt a friendly, a fraternal attitude towards the Ulster people … Let Sinn Fein assure [them] … that there is no desire for conquest or for ascendancy [and] that Ulstermen will be welcome to assist in the task of building up a new Ireland.[3]

In his second report to the Dáil cabinet (14 December) Fawsitt quoted extensively from this correspondence. He indicated that those he had interviewed in Belfast were 'ready to act on' the committee referred to by Williams. They 'but awaited the ratification of the Treaty', after which they would 'come together formally' to make 'their views known to' Craig and his ministers. He indicated that, if it was ratified, he would return to Belfast and have the committee 'called together … for the purpose mentioned'. While in the city, he said, he had been struck by the 'marked anti-British feeling' that had 'manifested itself'. He explained that 'this tendency is the outcome of Ulster's betrayal by her English allies'. He also repeated what the businessmen had told him: 'a friendly gesture from the Dáil towards Ulster would be most helpful just now'.[4]

Fawsitt next visited Belfast on 29 December, during the Dáil's Christmas recess and at the 'special request' of Michael Collins. His subsequent report to Dublin was markedly more subdued in tone. His 'impression' was that 'the proceedings in An Dáil had sobered down somewhat' the businesspeople's 'keenness on immediate action'. They had 'referred to the "extremist" speeches uttered' during the treaty debates, especially those by Seán MacEntee 'about Ulster and Ulster nationalists'. They had expressed 'disappointment at the apparent hesitancy' of deputies to accept the agreement 'in a spirit of goodwill'. Most of them stated that 'no progress towards a political settlement … could be attempted until the [Dáil's] decision

... was known, and a Provisional Government set up' under its terms. They still favoured Irish unity but, because of the strong opposition to the treaty, had 'decided to take no action at the time'. After it had been ratified, they agreed to 'consider ... approaching' Craig and indicating to him the 'advisability of arriving at an understanding' with the Free State. They again advised Fawsitt that a 'public statement by a responsible Southern leader' regarding the north would be 'timely and helpful'. They 'suggested' that he 'make an early return' to Belfast after the treaty issue was satisfactorily resolved.[5]

Fawsitt visited Belfast again between 11 and 13 January 1922, 'in compliance with' the Dáil cabinet's wishes and days after the treaty had been narrowly ratified. The only reference to the businessmen's committee in his fourth report (13 January) is that R.V. Williams, its 'organiser', was 'out of town'. But he records meeting Sam Kelly, one of its key figures and a prominent UUC member, and asking for his help in establishing contact with a representative of the Northern Ireland government. He outlined to him 'the substance of the conversation' he intended to hold with this individual. Subsequently Kelly met John Andrews, minister of labour, and 'reported' back to Fawsitt what he had said about Irish unity. Andrews stated that his government 'desired ... understanding and cooperation' with the south, but that its 'present mandate ... would not warrant a change in policy ... at the moment'. He indicated that the UUC's annual meeting was being held on 27 January, and that, 'pending [its] ... decision' on the issue, the Northern Ireland cabinet could 'take no steps towards an immediate arrangement' with the Free State. Kelly told Fawsitt that the businesspeople's committee would 'discuss the matter further', and 'take suitable action' after the UUC – 'of which all are members' – had met.[6]

Fawsitt and his interviewees had drawn encouragement over previous weeks from the emollient tone of some of Craig's speeches. When Winston Churchill, alarmed by the scale of rioting in Belfast, suggested that he meet Collins in London, he accepted. Afterwards, Craig explained to his cabinet and party his reasons for doing so. It was, he said, to ascertain the 'broad lines' of Sinn Féin policy, whether Collins 'intend[ed] to declare peace or war with Northern Ireland'. The three-hour conversation between them, which took place on 21 January, was cordial and wide ranging. The chasmic differences between their respective viewpoints only became evident when they met again 12 days later. When Fawsitt made his fifth and final visit to Belfast (on 25 January) it was to explain to Bishop Joseph MacRory the 'circumstances surrounding' the south's decision 'to lift provisionally the Belfast boycott'. This had been one of the points on which Craig and Collins reached agreement.[7]

By March 1922, 'North and South were to all intents and purposes openly at war.' The IRA campaign reached its climax in May. Between July 1920 and October 1922 civil disorder in Belfast claimed the lives of 498 of its citizens.[8] This was the outcome that Fawsitt and his associates had striven to prevent, but to attempt reconciliation then was to run counter to the temper of the times. Nonetheless, his newly discovered papers are, in Julitta Clancy's phrase, 'an eye-opener'. They confirm that political attitudes in the city, even during the 'troubles', were less intransigent and monolithic, more amenable and nuanced, than is often assumed.

The author wishes to express his gratitude to Julitta Clancy for her invaluable help in writing this article, and to the Clancy family for preserving the Fawsitt papers, and for making them available to the public for research purposes.

FURTHER READING

Long, Patrick. 'Fawsitt, Diarmaid (Jeremiah) (1884–1967), *Dictionary of Irish Biography*, https://www.dib.ie/biography/fawsitt-diarmuid-jeremiah-a3024 (accessed 2 Aug. 2021).
Parkinson, Alan, 2004. *Belfast's unholy war: the Troubles of the 1920s*. Dublin. Four Courts Press.

NOTES

[1] First report to Dáil cabinet, 3 Dec. 1921 (Cork County Archives (CCA), Diarmaid L. Fawsitt papers).
[2] Alec Wilson, Croglin, Ballyaughlis to Diarmaid Fawsitt, 7 Dec. 1921 (CCA, Fawsitt papers).
[3] Wilson to Fawsitt, n.d. (CCA, Fawsitt papers).
[4] Second report to Dáil cabinet, 14 Dec. 1921 (CCA, Fawsitt papers).
[5] Third report to Dáil cabinet, 31 Dec. 1921 (CCA, Fawsitt papers).
[6] Fourth report to Dáil cabinet, 13 Jan. 1922 (CCA, Fawsitt papers).
[7] Fifth report to Dáil cabinet, 25 Jan. 1922 (CCA, Fawsitt papers).
[8] Kieran Glennon, *From pogrom to civil war: Tom Glennon and the Belfast IRA* (Cork, 2013), 263.

Neurasthenia & Shell Shock

can be cured at home by using a delicious Emulsion of Olive Oil, Nature's Nerve Food.

The method of emulsifying the oil was invented last year by a Belfast man.

You can make the Emulsion at home in a few seconds. It will cure Sleeplessness in a week. Call or write for particulars.

HUGH LAMONT ORR, 17, GARFIELD ST., BELFAST.

Understanding 'trauma' in the 1920s

SÍOBHRA AIKEN

The establishment of Northern Ireland coincided with an explosion of interest in the nature of psychological injury. The return of thousands of soldiers from the First World War demanded the development of solutions for conditions such as 'shell-shock', 'hysteria' and 'exhaustion', along with other war neuroses. Civilians were not immune either. In Britain, 'neurasthenia' became known as 'the twentieth century disease'; it was the symptom of 'post-waritis' and 'the natural corollary to four years of war strain'.[1]

War did not end in Ireland in 1918, however. Revolution and partition were accompanied by uncertainty, sectarian violence and large-scale population displacement. These disturbances exposed civilians, ex-servicemen, activists, paramilitary groups and state forces alike to an array of experiences that could be characterised as 'traumatic'. But writing about 'trauma' in the context of the 1920s is not without its hazards. The current vocabulary of post-traumatic stress disorder did not enter medical discourse until 1980 and even now it remains a contested diagnosis. Oftentimes, as in the north of Ireland in the 1920s, medical understanding and treatment of psychological conditions reveals more about the conflicting political and social discourses of state and society than about the individual experience of trauma.

ARE YOU NERVOUS LIKE THIS?

If so, Curative Electricity Will Put You Right.

The Pulvermacher Appliances are the only inventions for the administration of curative electricity, endorsed by over fifty leading Doctors and by the official Academy, of Medicine in Paris.

she is travelling rapidly towards Nervous Exhaustion and Nervous Prostration.

HAVE YOU ANY OF THESE SYMPTOMS?

Are you Nervous, Timid, or Indecisive?
Do you lack Self-Confidence?
Do you dread open or closed spaces?
Are you wanting in Will Power?
Are you "fidgety," restless, or sleepless?
Do you blush or turn pale readily?
Do you shrink from strange company?
Are you subject to sudden impulses?
Do you crave for stimulants or drugs?

If so, you can safely assume that you are suffering from Neurasthenia. The neurasthenic also often suffer from **Indigestion, Liver Troubles, Constipation, Palpitation, Loss of Appetite, Excess of Appetite,** and a host of other disorders due to faulty functioning of various organs. Elec-

The Victoria Hospital for Diseases of the Nervous System, Paralysis and Epilepsy on Claremont Street, Belfast, was the first hospital of its kind in Ireland. Established in 1896, the hospital provided free treatment to male and female patients of all religious traditions, offering a favourable alternative to the workhouse 'lunatic ward'. By 1923 hospital management observed that 'nervous disease patients were an ever-growing class'. Hospital president Stephen Richardson attributed this rise to the 'late war and its after-effects', including unemployment, and pronounced that the 'whole body politic was feeling the strain of life'.[2]

The search for solutions for nervous conditions was fast becoming a competitive market. Throughout the 1920s Belfast crowds gathered for Londoner Miss Mary Stuart Glassford's many illustrated lectures on topics such as: 'Nervous breakdown, neurasthenia, neuritis: Causes and how to get well'. Advertisements appeared in Irish newspapers for Dr Cassell's Tablets, Ovaltine malt drinks and various electricity treatments, all promising quick solutions for conditions such as 'weak nerves'. There were more local remedies too: Hugh Lamont Orr, of 17 Garfield Street, sold a natural olive-oil-based 'nerve food' invented by a 'Belfast man'.[3] The Methodist weekly the *Irish Christian Advocate* promoted reading 'your Bible' to cure 'nervous prostration'.[4] Meanwhile, the National Sun Ray and Health Centre opened on 19 Arthur Street, Belfast, in 1928; the centre offered treatments for 'nerve-wrecked men and women' and promised to cure various 'diseases of darkness' such as deafness, infantile paralysis – and even baldness.

Though these advertisements suggest growing acceptance of mental illness, the emphasis on self-management points to the enduring shame associated with such ailments; these were conditions that should be quickly and discreetly remedied. The commercialisation of products for 'nerves' was also indicative of the fact that certain socioeconomic classes were more affected than others. In 1930 Dr Charles S. Thomson, medical superintendent officer of health for Belfast, outlined that 'neurasthenia' was 'common among brain-workers' such as teachers, barristers, clergymen, journalists and doctors. The 'rich woman' was particularly susceptible, although he contended that she would 'become free from morbid introspection and fanciful symptoms if she would go a-slumming'.[5]

The long-standing belief that nervous conditions were a 'female malady' is further evident in advertisements in the *Belfast Telegraph* that liken recovery from 'shattered nerves' to a process of remasculinisation: before/after images juxtapose the feeble and worn male body with the revitalised muscular man.[6] This idea of remasculinising returned soldiers had particular political implications in what was to become Northern Ireland. Whereas the shell-shocked soldier came to symbolise the futility of war in Britain, Jane G.V. McGaughey argues that members of the 36th Ulster Division of the British army were celebrated after the war as 'valiant unionist heroes'. This legacy of 'warrior manliness' was upheld by the USC, founded in October 1920, who were tasked with 'safeguard[ing] Ulster against the ever-increasing spectre of violence and social schism'.[7] The UVF Hospital at Craigavon treated 'neurasthenic' soldiers from 1917 and aimed to ensure the 'welfare of the brave men who are risking their lives in defence of the country'.[8]

Not all veterans were deemed deserving of this remasculinisation. In March 1922 it was brought to the attention of Winston Churchill that Catholic ex-servicemen at the hospital had been subject to 'anonymous correspondence' and 'personal threats'.[9] Such threats reflect the different treatment afforded to Catholic and nationalist returning soldiers by

WONDERFUL CURATIVE INVENTION.

ACCLAIMED BY SCIENTISTS THROUGHOUT THE WORLD.

OVERCOMES NEURASTHENIA AND ALL OTHER NERVOUS AILMENTS AND WEAKNESSES.

Amazing Reports Of Cures Confirmed By Medical Men All Over The Country.

comparison with their Protestant compatriots. This particular incident also highlights existing colonial prejudices, according to which the native Irish were predisposed to mental illness and not worthy, therefore, of remasculinisation. Indeed, higher levels of 'insanity' were registered among Irish ex-servicemen in the British army, although, as Joanna Bourke contends, this stereotype was not deemed applicable to Protestant Ulstermen.[10]

Republican activists intently sought to counter these colonial constructions of the Irish as effeminate and prone to mental illness. Although the Irish Grants Committee in London recognised 'shock' as a 'physical injury', the Military Service Pensions Board in Dublin was reluctant to recognise such 'diseases'. In their testimonies, IRA activists often stress how they maintained and overcame 'nerves'. For example, Tom McNally of the B Company Belfast Battalion recalled in an interview with Ernie O'Malley in 1949 that while Seamus Woods was 'sensitive', Roger McCorley was a 'fine fighter' who 'was cold like a fish. He had no nerves.'[11] Male veterans were sometimes more forthcoming about the nervous disposition of others than about their own emotional concerns; references to the nervous breakdowns of mothers, aunts or sisters often appear in men's testimonies as a means to draw attention to the psychological impact of conflict.

Gender, political and cultural concerns also played out in the treatment of 'nervous' patients. First World War veterans suffering from nerve diseases were afforded better treatment in the north than their counterparts in the south, where waiting lists were far longer than elsewhere in Britain. The course of treatment promoted at Craigavon was somewhat typical of the era: ex-servicemen were offered 'agreeable surroundings' and 'pleasant company'. Employment on the land was recommended to ensure the patient 'might be trained to again take his place in civil life'.[12] Meanwhile, Claremont Street Hospital in Belfast followed a particularly religious approach to treatment in the 1920s: while electrotherapy and curative work was endorsed, patients were also encouraged to join in communal worship and the hospital walls were adorned with religious texts.[13]

"Post-Waritis"
—the new disease and its remedy

Lowered vitality, "nervi-ness," and a general inability to "carry on"—these are the symptoms of "post-waritis" —the natural corollary to four years of war strain.

Really it is a mild form of neurasthenia—assisted perhaps by the recent influenza epidemic. What it means is that you are run-down and need a tonic.

You Need

SANATOGEN
THE GENUINE FOOD TONIC

Here is an interesting letter on the subject—from Miss Alice H. Cole, 29, Holland Park Avenue, London, W.:

Belfast News Letter

Emerging psychoanalytic approaches also informed medical management. Whereas medical records are often unclear regarding the exact nature of treatment, popular fiction is particularly revealing in terms of the currency of new ideas of psychoanalysis. In her 1922 novel, *Walk of a queen*, Cumann na mBan activist and nurse Annie M.P. Smithson promoted the view that, in the near future, 'suggestion and psychoanalysis will largely take the place of drugs'. Female activist Rosamond Jacob's novel *The troubled house* (written in the early 1920s) similarly points to the treatment of a male activist with a form of talk therapy after his involvement in the killings of Bloody Sunday in November 1920.

Indeed, the republican leader Michael Collins sent his men to the republican sympathiser and 'ladies' doctor' Dr Robert Farnan, who was known to 'cure by merely speaking to the men'.[14] The fact that Dr Farnan was a gynaecologist by profession but treated individuals for 'nervous exhaustion' underscores the contemporary belief that 'weak nerves' were inherently connected to the female body. The Military Service Pensions Board even had a policy of sending 'nervous' female applicants for gynaecological testing. These included Alice O'Rourke (*née* O'Byrne), who was considered to be 'neurasthenic' following two six-month terms of imprisonment in Armagh Gaol. O'Rourke was in charge of Cumann na mBan in the Banbridge district and oversaw an arms dump on her family land. She was arrested in possession of a revolver in 1922 and interned again in 1924 for possessing 'seditious literature'.[15]

But if Dr Farnan quickly 'cured' the men by speaking to them, and thus ensured their continued active duty, his treatment of female revolutionaries seems to have taken a different course. Female activist Siobhán Lankford recalled in her memoir *The hope and the sadness* (1980) that Dr Farnan prescribed her 'six weeks' complete rest in the Mater Hospital' followed by a period 'living in Malahide and Sutton' to treat her 'exhausted nerves'. This idea of 'complete rest' reflects the gender-specific 'rest cure' devised by Philadelphian neurologist Silas Weir Mitchell, which promoted a regime of mental and physical inactivity away from the patient's usual surroundings. Rest and change of environment was similarly recommended to Mrs Margaret Begley of Cregganbane, County Armagh. The wife of an ex-policeman, Margaret purportedly became 'unhinged' after a raid by 'armed men' on her home in October 1920. The raid was due to a dispute regarding turf cutting, exacerbated by Michael Begley's refusal to recognise the local Sinn Féin arbitration court. After being institutionalised in Armagh Lunatic Asylum, Margaret was advised that 'unless she got a prolonged period of rest in new surroundings the effects might become permanent'.[16]

The treatment recommended to Begley is at odds with the advice given to IRA brigadier-general Joseph O'Connor. Following a breakdown of 'nerves' in 1923, O'Connor was warned by his doctor not to go to the country as 'I would have to fight the thing in my ordinary surroundings.'[17] Whereas men's treatment was likened to a process of remasculinisation motivated towards social reintegration, women's treatment reinforced their exclusion from public life.

Trauma is popularly conflated with victimhood, but activists, paramilitaries and state forces also experienced psychological upset on account of acts they committed themselves. IRA man James Marron sought medical assistance after being involved in the atrocity in the Protestant village of Altnaveigh in south Armagh in June 1922: 'I could not sleep thinking of the woman and the others we shot.'[18] A war veteran and member of the USC was treated for hallucinations during the same period by Dr M.J. Nolan in Down County Mental Hospital. While the patient's condition was triggered by the 'explosion of a magazine', Nolan produced a remarkable report in which he foregrounded the psychological impact of the

Belfast News Letter

'Religio-Sexual-Political conflict' of those 'very stirring times'.[19] During the patient's six-day 'nightmare', he hallucinated that he was being pursued and tortured by imagined armies of insects – indicating, perhaps, memories of the First World War trenches. However, Nolan pinned the 'cause of all the trouble' on the patient's desire to marry a Catholic girl, Miss B., against his family's wishes. This dilemma was complicated by the suggestion that he may have fathered a child. The patient further imagined that he was attacked by a group of 'Irregulars' (IRA) in the form of 'small cockroaches' who came to shoot him for his role in the killing of their 'Colonel' – the father of Miss B.

Dr Nolan's emphasis on 'the stress of an acutely hostile environment' as central to his patient's condition was out of step with the published views of psychiatric professionals in Belfast. In 1925 Dr John Thompson of Claremont Street Hospital associated the rise in nervous patients with 'improper diet' and the 'evil of excessive tea drinking'.[20] In 1926 Mr Richardson condemned the 'inordinate love of pleasure and excitement connected with the cinema and liquor traffic'.[21]

Nolan's report was withheld, as Fiachra Byrne outlines, and not published until after his retirement in 1940.[22] It may have been easier to address the 'vices' of modern life than to reflect on the traumatic consequences of war, partition and communal strife.

FURTHER READING

Aiken, Síobhra, 2020 '"The women who had been straining every nerve": gender-specific medical management of trauma in the Irish Revolution (1916–1923)', in Melania Terrazas Gallego (ed.), *Trauma and identity in contemporary Irish culture*, 133–58. Bern. Peter Lang.

Bourke, Joanna, 2000 'Effeminacy, ethnicity and the end of trauma: the sufferings of "shell-shocked" men in Great Britain and Ireland, 1914–39', *Journal of Contemporary History*, vol. 35, no. 1, 57–69.

Byrne, Fiachra, 2017 'The report of a nightmare: hallucinating conflict in the political and personal frontiers of Ulster during the IRA border campaign of 1920–22', in David Durnin and Ian Miller (eds), *Medicine, health and Irish experiences of conflict 1914–45*, 109–24. Manchester. Manchester University Press.

Kelly, Brendan, 2016 *Hearing voices: the history of psychiatry in Ireland*. Kildare. Irish Academic Press.

Robinson, Michael, 2020 *Shell-shocked British army veterans in Ireland, 1918–39: a difficult homecoming*. Manchester. Manchester University Press.

NOTES

1 *Belfast News Letter*, 6 May 1919.
2 *Belfast News Letter*, 10 Nov. 1923.
3 *Belfast News Letter*, 18 May 1918.
4 'An unexpected prescription', *Irish Christian Advocate*, 13 May 1927.
5 *Belfast News Letter*, 22 Mar. 1930.
6 See Elaine Showalter, *The female malady: women, madness and English culture, 1830–1980* (New York, 1985); see *Belfast News Letter*, 5 Nov. 1923.
7 Jane G.V. McGaughey, 'The language of sacrifice: masculinities in Northern Ireland and the consequences of the Great War', *Patterns of Prejudice*, vol. 46, nos 3–4 (2012), 299.
8 *Belfast News Letter*, 17 Apr. 1917.
9 McGaughey, 'The language of sacrifice', 303.
10 Joanna Bourke, 'Effeminacy, ethnicity and the end of trauma: the sufferings of "shell-shocked" men in Great Britain and Ireland, 1914–39', *Journal of Contemporary History*, vol. 35, no. 1 (2000), 61.
11 Síobhra Aiken *et al.*, *The men will talk to me: Ernie O'Malley's interviews with the Northern Divisions* (Kildare, 2018), 107.
12 *Belfast News Letter*, 24 May 1917.
13 Ruth Baker, 'Claremont Street Hospital', *Ulster Tatler*, Jan. 1974, https://www.ums.ac.uk/inst/hcsh_rb.pdf (accessed 2 Aug 2021).
14 Col. Eamon Broy, Bureau of Military History (BMH) (Military Archives of Ireland (MAI), WS1285).
15 Alice O'Rourke, Military Service Pensions Collection (MSPC) (MAI, MSP34REF17007).
16 *Belfast News Letter*, 20 Jan. 1921, 19 Apr. 1921.
17 Joseph O'Connor, BMH (MAI, WS554).
18 James Marron, MSPC (MAI, DP3395).
19 M.J. Nolan, 'Commentary on a case of acute systematized hallucinosis (recorded by the patient as "the report of a nightmare")', *Journal of Mental Science*, vol. 86, no. 364 (Sep. 1940), 953–68.
20 *Belfast News Letter*, 14 Nov. 1925.
21 *Belfast News Letter*, 17 May 1926.
22 Fiachra Byrne, 'The report of a nightmare: hallucinating conflict in the political and personal frontiers of Ulster during the IRA border campaign of 1920–22' in David Durnin and Ian Miller (eds), *Medicine, health and Irish experiences of conflict 1914–45* (Manchester, 2017), 109–24.

2002/5/1

Secession or opting out?
Northern Ireland and Article 12
of the Anglo-Irish Treaty

DAVID TORRANCE

T R E A T Y .

between

GREAT BRITAIN & IRELAND.

signed

6th December, 1921.

at LONDON.

The parliament of Northern Ireland's decision to 'opt out' from the Irish Free State in December 1922 has received remarkably little attention. Perhaps this was because it was regarded as a *fait accompli*. The lack of scrutiny, however, has given rise to misunderstanding about what actually occurred in constitutional terms. Several historians have gone so far as claiming that Northern Ireland – in existence since May 1921 as a devolved part of the United Kingdom – 'seceded' from the Free State constituted on 6 December 1922. Brendan O'Leary has referred to 'a double secession': 'Ireland secedes from the union but the British insist that Northern Ireland, which they created in the 1920 act, will have the right to secede from Ireland, which the Sinn Féin negotiators accept.'[1]

Nicholas Mansergh also referred to Article 12 of the 1921 Anglo-Irish Treaty, which granted Northern Ireland an 'option to secede' from the Free State, while Dorothy Macardle wrote that it enabled the 'Six Counties to be detached from the Irish Free State'.[2] Paul Murray, meanwhile, referred to a 32-county free state 'provided for in the first ten articles of the Treaty' (as if they could somehow be read in isolation), with Articles 11 to 14 inclusive making 'provision for the dismemberment of this unit if the Northern Ireland Parliament desired that outcome'. More recently, a report from the Constitution Unit asserted that the treaty recognised Ireland 'as an all-island state', with Northern Ireland 'given the right to secede from the Irish Free State within one month'.[3]

In this view, Ireland was created whole in 1922 and subsequently 'dismembered' by the secession of its six north-eastern counties to rejoin the United Kingdom. In fact, the 1921 treaty created a 26-county free state with provision for it to expand to 32 counties after a period of one month, but only if Northern Ireland chose not to opt out. As Patrick Buckland put it, the treaty was 'a compromise between the ideal of Irish unity and the reality of Northern Ireland's position'.[4]

By the time of the July 1921 truce in the War of Independence, Northern Ireland had existed as a constitutional entity for seven months. Writing to Éamon de Valera on 20 July 1921, the UK prime minister, David Lloyd George, declared that any settlement 'must allow for full recognition of the existing powers and privileges of the Parliament and Government of Northern Ireland, which cannot be abrogated except by their own consent'.[5] This and other red lines were rejected by de Valera on 10 August. Negotiations, however, eventually began on 11 October.

On 26 October, the idea emerged of retaining the devolved parliament and government of Northern Ireland within the Free State, thus achieving the essential unity desired by the Sinn Féin plenipotentiaries. Lloyd George put this to Sir James Craig, the prime minister of Northern Ireland, twice in early November 1921, but he expressed his opposition. On 9 November, Arthur Griffith agreed to a boundary commission, which, it was suggested, might expand Free State territory beyond 26 counties.[6]

The following day Lloyd George tried again with Sir James, warning of 'grave difficulties' should Northern Ireland refuse to come under a Dublin parliament. Again Craig refused, which allowed Lloyd George to make his next move. On 12 November, the civil servant Tom Jones presented Griffith

Treaty between Great Britain and Ireland (6 Dec. 1921), NAI 2002/5/10.

with a proposal to 'create such Parliament for all Ireland, but to allow Ulster the right within a specified time on an address to the throne carried in both Houses of the Ulster Parliament, to elect to remain subject to the Imperial Parliament for all the reserved services'.[7] If the parliament of Northern Ireland elected to do so, then the *quid pro quo* would be the formation of a boundary commission. Believing this to be a tactical manoeuvre contrived to gain consent from Craig rather than a concrete solution, Griffith ended up agreeing to something more than he probably intended. This was formalised in a new draft of the treaty on 16 November. On 18 November Griffith realised what had transpired, although in the Irish delegates' response on 22 November, no concerns were raised.[8]

The temperature had cooled by 3 December. At a cabinet meeting in Dublin, de Valera said he could not agree to Northern Ireland having the option to 'contract out' of the Free State. In London the following day, Griffith stated his unhappiness with the northern clauses but, when Lloyd George met privately with Michael Collins, he convinced him that a boundary commission would result in the transfer of Tyrone and Fermanagh, as well as parts of Derry, Armagh and Down, to the Free State.[9]

In the UK cabinet room on 5 December 1921, Lloyd George pressed the Sinn Féin delegation to make a decision. With a dramatic flourish, he wielded the 13 November document to which Griffith had assented. The only point of negotiation was the length of time Northern Ireland would have to reach a decision. The Irish delegation suggested a month rather than a year and the prime minister agreed.[10] The treaty was agreed on 6 December 1921. Although Article 1 referred to 'Ireland' (rather than 'Southern Ireland'), the definition of the new Free State was qualified by Articles 11 and 12. Article 11 stated:

> [until] the expiration of one month from the passing of the Act of Parliament for the ratification of this instrument, the powers of the Parliament and the Government of the Irish Free State shall not be exercisable as respects Northern Ireland and the provisions of the Government of Ireland Act, 1920, shall so far as they relate to Northern Ireland remain of full force and effect.

And Article 12 stated:

> If before the expiration of the said month, an address is presented to His Majesty by both Houses of the Parliament of Northern Ireland to that effect, the powers of the Parliament and Government of the Irish Free

Treaty between Great Britain and Ireland (6 Dec. 1921), NAI 2002/5/10.

11.   Until the expiration of one month from the passing of the Act of Parliament for the ratification of this instrument, the powers of the Parliament and the government of the Irish Free State shall not be exercisable as respects Northern Ireland and the provisions of the Government of Ireland Act, 1920, shall, so far as they relate to Northern Ireland remain of full force and effect, and no election shall be held for the return of members to serve in the Parliament of the Irish Free State for constituencies in Northern Ireland, unless a resolution is passed by both Houses of the Parliament of Northern Ireland in favour of the holding of such election before the end of the said month.

12.   If before the expiration of the said month, an address is presented to His Majesty by both Houses of the Parliament of Northern Ireland to that effect, the powers of the Parliament and Government of the Irish Free State shall no longer extend to Northern Ireland, and the provisions of the Government of Ireland Act, 1920, (including those relating to the Council of Ireland) shall so far as they relate to Northern Ireland, continue to be of full force and effect, and this instrument shall have effect subject to the necessary modifications.

Provided that if such an address is so presented a Commission consisting of three persons, one to be appointed by the Government of the Irish Free State, one to be appointed by the Government of Northern Ireland and one who shall be Chairman to be appointed by the British Government shall determine in accordance with the wishes of the inhabitants, so far as may be compatible with economic and geographic conditions, the boundaries between Northern Ireland and the rest of Ireland, and for the purposes of the Government of Ireland Act, 1920, and of this instrument, the boundary of Northern Ireland shall be such as may be determined by such Commission.

State shall no longer extend to Northern Ireland, and the provisions of the Government of Ireland Act, 1920 ... shall, so far as they relate to Northern Ireland continue to be of full force and effect.

Article 14, meanwhile, contained what remained of essential unity. If no such address was presented, then the devolved institutions of Northern Ireland would continue as before, only under the Free State rather than Westminster. Ireland would be whole, but only if the parliament of Northern Ireland consented.

Although some of the language was ambivalent, the expression 'Ireland' in Article 1 of the treaty was, in the opinion of Brigid Hadfield, 'to be construed as excluding Northern Ireland, certainly in terms of United Kingdom law'. Indeed, the historian Ronan Fanning more bluntly judged Articles 11 and 12 as 'but fig leaves to cover the Irish negotiators' impotence to end partition'.[11]

Lloyd George was clear in a letter to Sir James Craig on 5 December 1921 that the government of Northern Ireland could either 'enter the Irish Free State' (at the end of the 'Ulster Month') or 'retain her present powers' as part of the UK (subject to revision of the boundary). There was no talk of secession. *The Times*'s summary of the treaty terms was also correct in stating that Northern Ireland was 'to have the option of remaining outside the Irish Free State'.[12]

Addressing the House of Commons on 14 December 1921, Lloyd George protested that 'endeavouring to persuade Ulster to come into an All-Ireland Parliament' had not amounted to 'coercion', something he and the former Conservative leader Andrew Bonar Law had pledged not to do at the 1918 general election and again in July 1921. Under the treaty, added Lloyd George:

Ulster has her option either to join an All-Ireland Parliament, or to remain exactly as she is. No change from her present position will be involved if she decides, by an Address to the Crown, to remain where she is.[13]

At this point, however, Sir James Craig appeared confused by the terms of the treaty, protesting in a letter to Lloyd George about the intention 'to place Northern Ireland automatically in the Irish Free State' (although he went on to acknowledge Ulster's 'right to contract out').[14] Craig appeared to be reading Articles 1 to 10 in isolation. Speaking in the Commons on 16 December, the Ulster Unionist MP Hugh O'Neill also referred to 'Ulster' having 'been nominally put into the Irish Free State, even though it may be for a very short period of time'.[15]

Hereafter, Ulster Unionists dropped their (arguably misplaced) complaint concerning automaticity and focused exclusively on the Boundary Commission. It was clear from parliamentary consideration of the Irish Free State (Agreement) Bill (which would, in part, ratify the agreement) that even some signatories to the treaty did not fully understand it. Winston Churchill, secretary of state for the colonies, claimed that if the 'Northern Government' exercised its 'option of contracting out of the Irish Free State' then 'the area of the Irish Free State is diminished accordingly'. In the Lords, the marquess of Salisbury had a better grip, stating that Article 11 provided 'that nothing shall come into force in Northern Ireland for a month after the Act of Parliament for the ratification of this instrument, and during that month Northern Ireland can specify its refusal to come into the Free State'.[16]

There was even more uncertainty as to when the so-called 'Ulster Month' was to begin. Lord Carson believed it ought to follow royal assent for the Irish Free State (Agreement) Bill, an interpretation shared by the provisional government in Dublin but not by the attorney general for England and Wales. Viscount Peel, the chancellor of the duchy of Lancaster, eventually made clear:

> the month will run not from the date when this Bill becomes an Act but from the date the second Bill establishing the Irish Constitution becomes an Act. The matter has been under discussion with the Irish Ministers and, although they took a different view themselves, it has been definitely agreed that the month should run from the date of the Act of Parliament establishing the Constitution.[17]

By August 1922 Arthur Griffith and Michael Collins were both dead and, a few months later, Lloyd George was no longer prime minister. Andrew Bonar Law, once again Conservative leader and now premier, removed any doubt regarding Conservative opposition by making it clear his government would ratify the treaty as intended. 'We are equally pledged,' he added, 'to safeguard the freedom of choice and the security of the Parliament and Government of Northern Ireland.'[18]

The Irish Free State (Constitution) Bill (which recognised the Free State constitution drafted in accordance with the treaty) was read for a second time on 27 November 1922 and moved by Bonar Law, who did not even mention Northern Ireland. The Irish Free State (Consequential Provisions) Bill was also considered that day. Its first clause dealt with:

the continued application of the [Government of Ireland] 1920 Act to Northern Ireland. In the event of Northern Ireland exercising its option and continuing outside the Free State, it is necessary, if that option be exercised, as it seems likely it will be, to have machinery ready for the legal continuance of the Northern Government.[19]

Both bills received royal assent on 5 December 1922 and, the following day, the Irish Free State was constituted by royal proclamation.

Meanwhile, in Belfast, the government of Northern Ireland and its advisers were taking no chances as regards the address required under Article 12 of the treaty. It was agreed this was to be treated like a bill, considered by both houses (which were due to meet on 12 December) and then submitted to the lord lieutenant, Viscount FitzAlan. Although Arthur Quekett, the parliamentary counsel, was clear that 'in law, Northern Ireland would not come in any respect within the Free State until the expiration of the Ulster month', Sir James Craig believed that 'any delay in voting out might lead to disturbances' and proposed bringing the meeting forward to 7 December. Whitehall was informed of the date change on 30 November.

Quekett also took considerable care to make sure that the form of the address would be treaty-compliant. An initial draft prayed that 'the powers of the Parliament and the Government of the Irish Free State *may not* extend to Northern Ireland', but by November this had been changed to '*shall no longer* extend' (emphasis added), which implied that at some point they would. Quekett acknowledged that this formulation was doubtless 'repugnant to popular feeling', but explained in a memo that they had been 'inserted on the opinion of the highest available legal authority to the effect that they are legally and formally necessary to ensure the validity of the Address' (in that Article 12 of the treaty used the same phrase).[20]

Sir James Craig was more than a little paranoid about the logistics. As 'a matter of precaution', he asked for two copies of the address to be certified by the clerk of parliament 'so that there may be no possible risk of trouble by one copy being lost'. Furthermore, he instructed the clerk to engross both copies on parchment '*before* Parliament meets' (emphasis added), something eased by advance notice of minor amendments likely to occur in the Senate. He also insisted that the address be presented to the lord lieutenant *and* the king the same day, lest someone argue that FitzAlan was insufficiently representative of the sovereign. Finally, Craig worried that two Ulster Unionist MPs might try to amend the address, a concern he passed on to the Commons speaker.[21]

Still, confusion reigned. On 7 December 1922, the day on which the parliament of Northern Ireland was due to exercise its Article 12 rights, *The Times* inaccurately referred to 'Belfast and the Six Counties' having formed 'part of the Free State of Ireland' since midnight on 6 December:

> There has not, one need hardly say, been any visible expression of the fact, and this curiosity of the Constitutional situation will not continue for more than another day at most.[22]

In the Dáil, meanwhile, President Cosgrave more accurately observed that it was 'not for him to anticipate the decision of the North Eastern Parliament on the question whether they would *join the South* on the terms of the Treaty' (emphasis added):

> Should they decide to cut themselves off from all contact with the Free State the South would regret very much such a decision ... Nevertheless, as they were perfectly entitled to take that course under the Treaty, the Free State was bound to respect such a decision in the event of its coming to pass.[23]

It took about half an hour for the Commons and the Senate of Northern Ireland to agree an address on which there was no division. It read:

> MOST GRACIOUS SOVEREIGN, We, your Majesty's most dutiful and loyal subjects, the Senators and Commons of Northern Ireland in Parliament assembled, having learnt of the passing of the Irish Free State Constitution Act, 1922, being the Act of Parliament for the ratification of the Articles of Agreement for a Treaty between Great Britain and Ireland, do, by this Humble Address, pray Your Majesty that the powers of the Parliament and Government of the Irish Free State shall no longer extend to Northern Ireland.[24]

Sir James Craig then personally transported two copies of the address to London via night boat and train. At 10.45 a.m. on Friday, 8 December he delivered one copy to Viscount FitzAlan. The lord lieutenant passed it on to the home secretary, William Bridgeman, whose officials had arranged for a courier to transport it by train to Sandringham. The courier departed Liverpool Street at 2.34 p.m. with a box containing the address and a draft reply and arrived at Wolferton at 5.29 p.m., from which he was conveyed to Sandringham. The king was shooting so was not presented with the address until later in the day. The second earl of Cromer, the lord chamberlain (of the Baring bank family), presented it on the home secretary's behalf.[25] The courier returned to London the following day, 9 December, with the box and the king's reply. Notice of both the address and the reply was ordered to be included in the *London Gazette* of 12 December 1922 'without fail'.[26]

On 13 December, Sir James Craig informed the (Northern Ireland) House of Commons that the monarch had responded as follows:

> I have received the Address presented to me by both Houses of the Parliament of Northern Ireland in pursuance of Article 12 of the Articles of Agreement set forth in the Schedule to the Irish Free State (Agreement) Act, 1922, and of Section 5 of the Irish Free State Constitution Act, 1922; and I have caused my Ministers and the Irish Free State Government to be so informed.[27]

Earlier, Sir James had referred to 'exercising our old determination to vote ourselves out of the Free State and form an entity of ourselves'.[28] He had done no such thing. Northern Ireland had not spent a single day under the jurisdiction of the Free State and had maintained the constitutional status quo by resolving *not to join* the new dominion within the stipulated 'Ulster Month'. This meant the Free State, born as a 26-county entity on 6 December 1922, would not encompass all 32 counties as of 6 January 1923. The parliament of Northern Ireland had 'opted' or 'contracted out' of its future inclusion in an all-Ireland parliament. It had not 'seceded' from the Irish Free State for the simple reason – as clearly expressed in the 1921 treaty – that it had never formed part of it.

FURTHER READING

Buckland, Patrick, 1981 *A history of Northern Ireland*. Dublin. Gill and Macmillan.

Fanning, Ronan, 2013 *Fatal path: British government and Irish revolution 1910–1922*. London. Faber and Faber.

Hadfield, Brigid, 1989 *The constitution of Northern Ireland*. Belfast. SLS Legal Publications.

Mansergh, Nicholas, 1991 *The unresolved question: the Anglo-Irish settlement and its undoing, 1912–72*. New Haven. Yale University Press.

Murray, Paul, 2011 *The Irish Boundary Commission and its origins, 1886–1925*. Dublin. UCD Press.

Pakenham, Frank (Lord Longford), 1921 (1972 ed.) *Peace by ordeal: an account, from first-hand sources, of the negotiation and signature of the Anglo-Irish Treaty 1921*. London. Sidgwick and Jackson.

NOTES

[1] 'Inside politics: the centenary of Northern Ireland', *The Irish Times* podcast, 12 Feb. 2021.

[2] Nicholas Mansergh, *The unresolved question: the Anglo-Irish settlement and its undoing, 1912–72* (New Haven, 1991), 220; Dorothy Macardle, *The Irish republic* (London, 1937 (1968 ed.)), 749.

[3] Paul Murray, *The Irish Boundary Commission and its origins, 1886–1925* (Dublin, 2011), 97; *Working Group on Unification Referendums on the Island of Ireland final report, May 2021* (London, 2021), para 2.8.

[4] Patrick Buckland, *A history of Northern Ireland* (Dublin, 1981), 38.

[5] *Correspondence relating to the proposals of His Majesty's government for an Irish settlement*, Cmd 1502 (London, 1921).

[6] Frank Pakenham (Lord Longford), *Peace by ordeal: an account, from first-hand sources, of the negotiation and signature of the Anglo-Irish Treaty 1921* (London, 1921 (1972 ed.)), 156; Ronan Fanning, *Fatal path: British government and Irish revolution 1910–1922* (London, 2013), 293.

[7] Pakenham, *Peace by ordeal*, 177–8.

[8] Ibid., 253.

[9] Ibid., 221.

[10] Ibid., 255.

[11] Brigid Hadfield, *The constitution of Northern Ireland* (Belfast, 1989), 35; Fanning, *Fatal path*, 314.

[12] *The Times*, 8 and 16 Dec. 1921.

[13] *Hansard 5 (Commons)*, vol. 149 (14 Dec. 1921), cols 38–40.

[14] *The Times*, 16 Dec. 1921.

[15] *Hansard 5 (Commons)*, vol. 149 (16 Dec. 1921), col. 312.

[16] *Hansard 5 (Commons)*, vol. 151 (6 Mar. 1922) col. 910, (9 Mar. 1922), col. 409.

[17] *Hansard 5 (Lords)*, vol. 49 (9 Mar. 1922), col. 420.

[18] *The Times*, 27 Oct. 1922.

[19] *Hansard 5 (Commons)*, vol. 159 (27 Nov. 1922), col. 388.

[20] PRONI, CAB6/76.

[21] Ibid.

[22] *The Times*, 7 Dec. 1922.

[23] Ibid.

[24] PRONI, CAB6/76.

[25] It is unclear what became of the two parchment copies of the address, although PRONI, CAB6/76 records that on 16 December 1922 the East Antrim MP George B. Hanna was sent a copy 'of the Address opting us out of the Free State duly signed by the Prime Minister'.

[26] For the logistics of the address and its presentation to the king, see TNA, HO45/12359.

[27] *Belfast Gazette*, 15 Dec. 1922.

[28] *The Times*, 8 Dec. 1922.

A border vignette
The Belleek–Pettigo
events of June 1922

MARGARET O'CALLAGHAN

The Belleek–Pettigo episode on the new Irish border, culminating on 8 June 1922, is well documented.[1] It is often represented as a moment during which Winston Churchill interfered in defence of the new Craig government in Belfast against the alleged, and in this case actual, proto-invasions of Provisional Government and Anti-Treaty troops. In the classic representation of the incident in Tom Jones's *Whitehall Diary*, Churchill, manoeuvring for advantage with the Conservative Party and anxious to curry favour with his unionist base, overcame the sensible reservations of Lloyd George and Jones and sent in British troops.[2] This followed a day of Jones and Lloyd George complaining about Churchill's disloyalty to all colleagues at all times and Churchill's appropriation of the role of leader of a revolt of Tory die-hards against Lloyd George. On the eve of the post-Treaty 'southern' elections, matters were fraught and tense. Tom Jones wanted to keep Michael Collins and Arthur Griffith in the loop on what was happening, but Churchill vetoed that possibility.

We know that Churchill was deeply embroiled in Northern Irish matters in 1922. He was setting up meetings between James Craig and Michael Collins and bombarding Collins in particular with advice and nudges, frequently by telegram. Pettigo represents the high point of his support for the Craig project and a hardening of his determination to insist that in Dublin the Provisional Government take immediate action against their IRA opponents in the Four Courts.[3]

That shift of focus from the border to the start of the Civil War in Dublin, through the attack on Rory O'Connor and the IRA in the Four Courts at Churchill's insistence, mirrors Churchill's own shifting strategic grip on the situation. In the first months of 1922 things did not look good for Craig. Having secured the establishment of his Northern Ireland through the apparently watertight Government of Ireland Act, and having designed its composition as six rather than four or nine counties, by the summer of 1921 he might have been entitled to relax. But the terms of the Anglo-Irish Treaty of December 1921 put all his gains in jeopardy.

The Treaty was allegedly negotiated by representatives of Ireland. Where, then, did that leave the newly established Northern Ireland? And why was this entity, established under the Government of Ireland Act, seemingly required to opt out of the Irish Free State if it was already in existence? In addition, the Treaty provided for a Boundary Commission that could revise the limits of this new and now more precarious polity. If the local government elections of 1920, run on a proportional-representation basis, were anything to go by, a putative future boundary commission could, if taking into account the 'wishes of the inhabitants' (even if also considering 'economic and geographic considerations'),[4] return Tyrone, Fermanagh, Derry city, Newry and south Armagh to Dublin. All of these areas had nationalist majorities.

In the 1920 local elections, nationalists had done well in Fermanagh, Tyrone and Derry city, and left-wing Labour Unionists had done well in Belfast. None of this augured well for the possible outcome of soliciting the 'wishes of the inhabitants'. Much of Craig's behaviour in the first half of 1922 can be understood in the context of his steely determination to preserve what he had in the full awareness that his title deeds were less secure than he had imagined.

Writing from his Belfast home, 'Cloreen', on 5 June 1922, Fred Crawford issued dire warnings to Craig about the dangers of their position. He feared Lloyd George was 'working with Ulster's two arch enemies [Nevil] Macready and [John] Anderson', who 'will then give way to Collins', and disliked the fact that it now appeared British troops had taken control of the border. Responding, W.B. Spender, the incredibly assiduous northern cabinet secretary, replied to Crawford that Craig was in London, where we know he had excellent access to Churchill.[5]

On the previous Tuesday, at Belleek, a local Church of Ireland clergyman, had asked for what he called relief. He saw local commander of the USC, Sir Guy Richardson, and Basil Brooke, who 'could do nothing'.[6] Lieutenant Colonel W.H. Barton, JP, owner of the Waterfoot House at Pettigo, wrote a full account of the beginnings of one aspect of the affair. His report, clearly intended for the official record and solicited by Spender, is said to be an account 'from 10am 29 May to midnight on 3 or 4 June 1922'.[7] It is an important document, as it narrates some of the events that precipitated the Churchill intervention, illuminates the mentalities of local unionists, the cross-class alliances forged through the local gentry that tied them in to Craig. It is a story of local men and their actions. It reads as follows:

> Robert Watson arrived from Castle Caldwell by bicycle looking for a
> doctor to attend Aiken who was wounded there. I went with George Fyfe
> to ferry Robert Watson across the mouth of the Pettigo Waterfoot Rivers
> from Fermanagh to Fermanagh so that he would not have to cross
> Donegal territory. On the way to the boathouse I saw armed men on the
> Donegal side of the Waterfoot River. One of them was aiming a rifle at us
> from behind a tree. He dropped undercover and retired to the Waterfoot
> house. We armed and on coming out saw a number of men crossing the
> Waterfoot river from the Donegal side to the Fermanagh side[.] I fired on
> them [and] they retired unhurriedly and fired one shot back.
>
> We remained at the Waterfoot House from Monday to Saturday being
> constantly fired on. On approaching my boathouse accompanied by Mr
> John Graham of Aughnablaney we were fired out at about 100 yards from
> a trench constructed at the apex of the Co. Donegal at the junction of the
> Waterfoot and and Pettigo rivers. [8]

Barton left them on Friday night and was replaced by a Corporal Pitt, who
was to 'bring around British troops'. Pitt reported that on Saturday, 3 June
at about 3 p.m., heavy fire was trained on Waterfoot House 'from the
Donegal side' and, 'having only one man left' and 'believing they were about
to advance', he stole up under cover to within 200 yards of one of their
trenches and fired into it. Barton was keen to emphasise throughout his
statement, forwarded to Craig for dissemination, that except for 'those 5
rounds fired by Corporal Pitt in reply to the fire from Donegal' and the
retaliatory fire he trained on those trying to cross what he interestingly calls
'the county boundary', all of the negative initiations were allegedly from the
southern side.[9]

On 6 June 1922, the county commandant of the Specials in Tyrone,
Brigadier-General Ambrose Ricardo, wrote from the Ulster Club in Belfast
to Craig's private secretary, C.H. Blackmore, of a similar situation on the
Tyrone–Donegal border near Strabane and Lifford. Strabane Station on the
Tyrone side is 700 yards from Lifford Bridge in Donegal. Ironically, Strabane,
on the northern side of the new border, was reported to have 'nearly 5,000
inhabitants with a R.C. majority'. Ricardo described Lifford in Donegal as
having a Protestant majority – 'Many Strabane businessmen live there.'
There, apparently, everything had been 'very peaceful until last weekend'. He
noted that, on the Donegal side, 'IRA Free State men occupy the old RIC
barracks in Lifford', but 'IRA Republicans have been moving into the area
gradually'.[10]

It appears that the Lifford–Strabane area had established a local
conciliation committee. There was a nationalist majority on the urban council

and there was one National Labour representative on the committee, with four clergymen of different denominations. Ricardo only named 'the Rev J. Baird, Rev S. Clark, myself' and someone he called 'Peter O'Donnell' (anti-Treaty). This was Peadar O'Donnell, the well-known socialist republican. Ricardo sent huge chunks of O'Donnell's statements on an Irish republic and his equal dislike of the Belfast and Dublin governments up to Belfast.

James Craig replied to Ricardo, apologising for not getting his account of local events sent on to London, as he had clearly assumed they would be:

> should have sent it to the PM in England to show to Mr Churchill, but I do not like to do this without your consent nor could I guarantee that the Imperial authorities would keep confidential any list of names, unless omitted this in making a copy.[11]

What is apparent is that an array of local information was being forwarded to London, some via Lloyd George and much directly to Churchill. The contrast between the Lifford–Strabane situation and that of Belleek–Pettigo was intended to demonstrate to London that the north's problems were a product of southern interference, and that Craig's government needed greater protection, support, military hardware and money to survive. This explains Craig's presence in London during some of these crucial days and the advantage of purchasing a spacious and grand London house. Interestingly, however, there was little agreement between Crawford and Craig on how to proceed.

Further extensive and detailed information on Pettigo was conveyed to Wilfrid Spender and passed on politically in London and to the editor of the *Belfast Evening Telegraph*. Thomas Moles, the Unionist MP for South Belfast at both Westminster and Stormont, showed some unease at the nature of newspaper reporting generally at the time, though from what perspective is unclear. Spender collected evidence about other local unionists in Pettigo, emphasising their need for protection from attack from across the bridge. Edgar McKegney from Pettigo wrote to Spender to say that Protestants in the townlands of Cashelenny and Grousehall were forced to leave their farms. In Tyrone, Colonel Richardson of the Rossfad area, commandant of the local Specials, endorsed statements about local disruption, where 'letters are held up' as 'the postmaster at Omagh is a bitter Sinn Feiner'.[12]

On 14 June Michael Collins was in talks with the former military commander in Ireland and occasional presence at the Treaty negotiations, General Sir Nevil Macready, on the situation in Garrison and Kesh. As a result of all of this, a commission for the border (separate from and not directly related to the Boundary Commission) was appointed. It was established at 12 noon on 14 June 1922. The meeting was between Macready, Michael Collins, Andy Cope (a crucial Dublin Castle operator) and Commandant Hogan. A record of the agreement was sent to the chief of the Imperial General Staff at the War Office, Whitehall.

The Border Commission was a liaison body that operated on both sides of the border and reported directly to a British army superior at GHQ Ireland, Parkgate, Dublin. It consisted of unarmed police from both sides who were to wear the 'same brassard'. It was much approved by James Cooper, Brook View, Enniskillen. It was announced, 'If this experiment is successful it shall be extended to other parts of the border.' But June was a crucial turning point and Churchill's role both on the border and in Dublin over the following two weeks changed the agenda of partition, perhaps irrevocably.[13]

FURTHER READING

Jones, Thomas (Keith Middlemas, ed.), 1971
    Whitehall Diary: vol. iii, Ireland 1918–1925.
    London. Oxford University Press.
Kinsella, Anthony, 1997 'The Pettigo–Belleek
    triangle incident', *The Irish Sword*, vol. 20,
    346–66.
Magill, Christopher, 2020 *Political conflict in
    east Ulster, 1920–1922: revolution and
    reprisal.* Woodbridge. Boydell Press.
O'Callaghan, Margaret, 2006 'Genealogies of
    partition: history, history-writing and "the
    Troubles" in Ireland', *Critical Review of
    International Social and Political Philosophy*,
    vol. 9, 619–34.

NOTES

[1] Anthony Kinsella, 'The Pettigo–Belleek
    triangle incident', *The Irish Sword*, vol. 20
    (1997), 346–66 (1997), 346–66; John B.
    Cunningham, 'The Struggle for the
    Belleek–Pettigo Salient, 1922', *Donegal
    Annual*, 34 (1982), 38–59.
[2] Thomas Jones, *Whitehall Diary: vol. iii,
    Ireland 1918–1925* (Keith Middlemas, ed.,
    London, 1971), 212.
[3] See Kevin Matthews, *Fatal Influence: the
    impact of Ireland on British politics,
    1920–1925* (Dublin, 2004), 71–81.
[4] Margaret O'Callaghan, 'Old parchment and
    water: the Boundary Commission of 1925
    and the copper fastening of the Irish border',
    Bullan: An Irish Studies Journal, vol. 4, no. 2
    (2000), 27–55.
[5] PRONI, CAB/9/Z/1/2.
[6] Brian Barton, *Brookeborough: the making of
    a prime minister* (Belfast, 1988). Brooke
    already had control of over a hundred
    Specials, and a boat.
[7] PRONI, CAB/9/Z/1/2.
[8] Ibid.
[9] Ibid.
[10] Ibid.
[11] Ibid.
[12] Ibid.
[13] Ibid

(ORIGINAL CAPTION): A scene in the streets of Belleek, Ulster, shortly
after that town had been recaptured and occupied by Royal Irish
infantry, supported by armored [sic] cars (23 June 1922).

(BETTMANN/CONTRIBUTOR) GETTY IMAGES

Tragedies and farce
Partition and the border

PETER LEARY

NATIONAL LIBRARY OF IRELAND

Leaflet No. 4. NLC 99

British Electors! Uphold the Treaty!

STUDY THIS MAP.

Map showing the political complexion of the areas governed by the Belfast Parliament according to the last Rural District Elections.

Under the Treaty between Great Britain and Ireland signed on the 6th December, 1921, the Six Counties of the Belfast Parliament **still belong to the Irish Free State.** They are allowed one month from the date of the final ratification of the Treaty within which they can elect to go out of the Free State. If and when they so choose Clause 12 of the Treaty provides that:—

"**A Commission consisting of three persons, one to be appointed by the Government of the Irish Free State, one to be appointed by the Government of Northern Ireland, and one, who shall be chairman, to be appointed by the British Government, shall determine in accordance with the wishes of the inhabitants,** so far as may be compatible with economic and geographic conditions, **the Boundaries between Northern Ireland and the rest of Ireland.**"

Belfast wants you to break this vital Clause of the Treaty by forcing hundreds of thousands of people favourable to the Free State to remain under her Parliament.

All that Ireland wants is:—

LEAVE THE BOUNDARY QUESTION TO BE DETERMINED BY THE INHABITANTS AS LAID DOWN IN THE TREATY.

ELECTORS! UPHOLD THE TREATY!

Printed by Alex. Thom & Co., Ltd., Tone Printing Works, Botanic Road, Dublin.

North East Boundary
Bureau, Leaflet, no. 4, ILB
300 p 6 [Item 99].

In early July 1923, Joseph Johnston travelled north to visit the border towns of Swanlinbar, County Cavan, and Clones, County Monaghan. A Presbyterian from rural Tyrone and a lecturer at Trinity College, Dublin, Johnston had been appointed by fellow northerner and Tyrone Catholic Kevin O'Shiel to advise the Irish Free State government and its North East Boundary Bureau on the economic impacts of partition in anticipation of the Irish Boundary Commission.[1]

Violence had recently shaken both communities. On 11 February 1922, an unplanned confrontation in Clones between members of the IRA stationed in the town and an armed party of uniformed USC, who were travelling by train from Newtownards via Belfast to Enniskillen, resulted in an 'affray' or, as others would have it, 'massacre', that left four constabulary and the local IRA commandant dead and many wounded. Three months prior to Johnston's visit to Swanlinbar, on Holy Thursday, 29 March 1923, the battered body of 19-year-old aspiring teacher, Martha Teresa Lunney, had been discovered 'about three yards from the boundary between Cavan and Fermanagh'. On the northern or Kinawley side, it was not much further from her parents' home and only a short walk from the village. This brutal rape and murder – this border 'outrage' in the euphemistic language of the time – horrified the local populace. Although a party of policemen from Kinawley were in the vicinity, suspicion between the RUC and Civic Guard on either side of the boundary line may have marred the subsequent investigation and no perpetrator was ever found. But the published lists of attendees at her funeral and condolences received suggest that some things could still transcend the social wounds onto which several years of conflict had poured so much salt. From north and south, all religious and political creeds were briefly brought together in sympathy with the Lunneys and in sorrow for their troubles.[2]

On 1 April 1923, the day immediately after Martha Lunney's funeral, the boundary next to which her body was found became a customs border. The main road from Swanlinbar to Enniskillen was one of 16 border crossings approved for trade in dutiable goods. It was from there that the town's merchants were used to buying 'beer, stout, spirits, meal, flour, groceries, provisions, [and] hardware', and selling 'eggs, poultry and other agricultural produce', but, when Johnston visited in July, that trade had almost stopped. The principal route had remained closed since the previous March, when 'a bridge about 200 yards on the Northern side of the border' was destroyed. Repeated attempts by local people to reopen the crossing had been thwarted by the Specials and, since June, 'a mountain bye road' used by light traffic was also closed. On one occasion, according to Johnston's sources, local workers were brought 'in handcuffs to the spot and compelled [to assist in] the destruction'.

In Clones, he heard a similar story. South of that town, 'practically all of the roads crossing the border' had been 'rendered impassable' in the weeks following the 'affray' in 1922, either by trenching, the destruction of bridges or being 'barricaded with trees and stones'. [3] For more than a year farmers and other residents had faced long detours when travelling not just into Northern Ireland but also to Clones itself and south to Cavan town as a number of important local roads cross the border several times.

In both places, attempts were made to keep the border open. At Annie Bridge, near Clones, access to a turf bog had been maintained by the construction of a ford across the river but it too had since been blocked by barbed wire, under orders from 'a Kerry Roman Catholic' who commanded the Specials at Newtownbutler. At Swanlinbar, goods from Enniskillen came by lorry as far as the broken bridge, where they were 'transhipped' to awaiting vehicles on the other side. A 'Separating Station for milk' continued to receive supplies of milk from both sides of the border but, whereas it had formerly provided cream to a central creamery at Kinawley in County Fermanagh, about seven miles away, '[it] now [had] to send the cream, some 30 miles distance, to Killeshandra in Co. Cavan'.[4]

From the early 1920s onwards, living in close proximity to the border meant dislocation, uncertainty and often danger. Shopping, visiting family or travelling to a place of worship, or later to the bingo or a dance, could be complicated by customs restrictions, security policies and even questions of nationhood and identity.

Based on historic county boundaries, the border dissected around 200 roads and some 1,400 land holdings, at least one village, several houses and other buildings. The village of Pettigo, with fewer than 400 inhabitants, was divided by the River Termon, which marked the border running through it. The Drummully salient, a small area consisting of 16 townlands and home to 60 families in the Free State, was left completely inaccessible by road or rail except through Northern Ireland. At Gortineddan, between Derrylin, County Fermanagh, and Ballyconnell, County Cavan, John and Margaret Murray and their family could sit in a chair in one state while eating from a table in the other, as the border ran right through the middle of their house.[5]

The Irish Boundary Commission, for which Johnston's visit was intended to prepare, might have resolved some of these anomalies. Its collapse towards the end of 1925 left them and the boundary line in place. The witnesses who appeared at its hearings in the spring and summer of that year described how partition had already impacted their lives. Many lamented the 'natural' connections between Derry and Donegal, which had been severed, and those of smaller towns and villages like Aughnacloy in County Tyrone with its long-standing hinterland in adjacent County Monaghan. John Simms of Lifford, County Donegal, told of 'the performances going on' at the bridge separating that town from neighbouring Strabane, County Tyrone, complaining, 'If you send your wife out for a herring, she has to cross the Customs boundary.'[6]

Not only Ireland, but also the province of Ulster, was divided. So too were more local markers of identity and belonging. The rival and often overlapping spiritual units – parishes and dioceses – frequently crossed the county lines, as did other administrative spaces including poor-law unions and urban and rural district council areas. As the Church of Ireland minister of one partitioned parish put it, 'We never thought about the difference between one county and another before that change was made.'[7]

Import levies had been placed on products ranging from boots and clothes to strong drink, planks of wood and other hardware, but most farm produce remained exempt from duty. Clothing that was worn while crossing, and even alcohol and tobacco 'for use on the journey', could pass over without charge. Lydia Cunningham, a widow from the Inishowen Peninsula and one of very few women to give evidence to the commission, stressed that while you might get groceries 'quite well' in nearby Buncrana, for anything else 'you would not get the same quality of goods as one is accustomed to'. Mrs Wilson, a former schoolteacher from Raphoe in Donegal, told how for 'anything of a superior class' she still crossed the border to shop in Derry, while Alexander Leckey, a Presbyterian minister in his seventies, complained of having to go 'into a foreign country' to buy a suit in the latest fashion as the local outlets were simply 'not up-to-date'.[8]

Statements such as these highlight, on the one hand, that the border ruptured old connections but, on the other hand, that it still needed to be crossed. The cut could never be complete. By December 1924 at least one member of the Specials was again content to risk changing trains at Clones when travelling home to Belfast from Fermanagh and both the rail and road networks continued to traverse the boundary.[9] The advent of the customs barrier saw border road crossings divided into three types. The 16 approved routes were equipped with customs facilities and were the only roads by which dutiable items, including motor vehicles, could legally be brought in or out. Most of the remainder were classed as 'unapproved'. These could be used solely for exempt farm produce and those not carrying goods provided they travelled by foot, bicycle or horse-drawn vehicle. In addition, a handful of concession roads permitted journeys between two places in the south or two places in the north that passed through the other jurisdiction on the way.

However practical some of these arrangements were, they could also generate frustration. Residents of Cullaville in south Armagh who wished to travel by car to nearby Castleblayney, and stay within the law, were obliged by the rules 'to set off in the opposite direction' to reach an approved crossing and had their passes stamped. Having legally crossed the border once, they had to join the concession route (coming from Dundalk) and travel back through their own village without stopping, because traffic using that road was not permitted to stop as it passed through Northern Ireland.[10]

Opportunity and necessity would soon give rise to new incentives for border crossing. Differences in prices and periods of hardship, rationing and shortages fuelled a flourishing smuggling economy. Anglo-Irish trade disputes during the 1930s saw livestock driven north in large numbers. When the Second World War broke out in 1939, contraband became almost ubiquitous. By 1942, one hapless official in Dundalk felt compelled to write to his superiors about the Northern Ireland women who flooded into the town every Sunday on the cross-border train:

> There is ... an urgent need of women searchers on the Customs Staffs, as ... housewives ... are the principal offenders. Men searchers are helpless. On several occasions ... at Dundalk Station women have told Customs men that they had butter and dared them to get it.[11]

Determined more by force than by democratic principles, the territorial dimensions of Northern Ireland extended far beyond the hinterlands of Belfast and the location of the boundary rarely functioned as an interface between unionist and nationalist communities. More often, it bisected districts that were demographically and politically similar. Catholic preponderance, interspersed with Protestant concentrations, was broadly characteristic of the borderlands in both jurisdictions and it was in these majority nationalist border areas of Northern Ireland that municipal discrimination against that community was consistently most acute. In the 1920s and 1950s and again from the early 1970s, attempts to close the unapproved crossings were resisted by local people who filled holes, mended bridges and removed barriers. 'Even men who had never been reputed for their addiction to hard work,' remarked one witty observer in November 1971, 'seemed to get a new lease of life when it came to repairing this kind of damage'; 'Life,' he insisted, 'must go on'.[12]

As the sun set on the twentieth century, some of the pain, irritation and fury of partition seemed to dim. European integration and then the peace process led first to the disappearance of the customs barrier and then to the removal of military installations and the opening up of many long-closed border crossings. In a variant of what has recently been described as 'disremembering', it became possible to pass from one political jurisdiction to another while forgetting, or at least neglecting to remember, the troubles of the past and even the fact that a border had been crossed. By the dawn of this millennium the border was more permeable than at any point since 1922 but, while Martha Lunney's name was still remembered, her story was recounted only with reluctance and 'in hushed tones' in Swanlinbar.[13] The border regions continue to be shaped by bonds and impulses that sustain and pull together as well as ones that break and wedge apart. The recent Brexit

Monument to the 'BorderBusters' at Gortoral, County Fermanagh,
a short distance outside Swanlinbar, County Cavan.

PETER LEARY

debates have reminded everyone of the ongoing presence of the border and, as partition reaches its centenary, its future, as ever, looks uncertain. Whether or not the border survives for another hundred years, it has marked the lives of border communities for generations.

FURTHER READING

Beiner, Guy, 2018 *Forgetful remembrance: social forgetting and vernacular historiography of a rebellion in Ulster*. Oxford. Oxford University Press.
Harvey, Brian *et al.*, 2005 *The emerald curtain: the social impact of the Irish border*. Carrickmacross. Triskele Community Training and Development.
Leary, Peter, 2018 'A house divided: the Murrays of the border and the rise and decline of a small Irish house', *History Workshop Journal*, vol. 86, 269–90.
Leary, Peter, 2016 *Unapproved routes: histories of the Irish border, 1922–1972*. Oxford. Oxford University Press.
Lynch, Robert, 2004 'The Clones affray, 1922: massacre or invasion?', *History Ireland*, vol. 12, no. 3, 33–7.
Whyte, John, 1983 'How much discrimination was there under the Unionist regime, 1921–1968?', in Tom Gallagher and James O'Connell (eds), *Contemporary Irish Studies*, 1–35. Manchester. Manchester University Press.

NOTES

[1] National Archives of Ireland (NAI), TSCH/3/S3161, S4743.
[2] Robert Lynch, 'The Clones affray, 1922: massacre or invasion?', *History Ireland*, vol. 12, no. 3 (2004), 33–7; PRONI, FER/6/1/1/5/12, HA/5/328; *Freeman's Journal*, 4 Apr. 1923; *Anglo-Celt*, 12 May 1923.

[3] NAI, TSCH/3/S3161.

[4] Ibid.

[5] Brian Harvey *et al.*, *The emerald curtain: the social impact of the Irish border* (Carrickmacross, 2005), 40; Peter Leary, 'A house divided: the Murrays of the border and the rise and decline of a small Irish house', *History Workshop Journal*, vol. 86 (autumn 2018), 269–90.

[6] Irish Boundary Commission, Donegal County, Protestant Registration Association, vol. 3, evidence of Mr John F.A. Simms, 27 May 1925 (TNA, CAB 61/53).

[7] Irish Boundary Commission, unionist inhabitants of Drummully Parish, evidence of Reverend J.R. Meara, 4 May 1925 (TNA, CAB 61/56).

[8] Irish Boundary Commission, Irish Free State Customs Service, evidence of Mr O'Golain, 19 June 1925 (TNA, CAB 61/76); evidence of Mrs Lydia Cunningham, Mrs Wilson and Reverend A.G. Leckey, 26–7 May 1925 (TNA, CAB 61/53).

[9] *Weekly Irish Times*, 13 Dec. 1924. I am extremely grateful to Tim Wilson for bringing this to my attention.

[10] W.F. Stout to S.H.E. Burley, 20 Nov. 1962 (PRONI, CAB/9/G/73/11); *Irish News*, 3 Aug. 1963.

[11] NAI, JUS/90/110/4.

[12] John Whyte, 'How much discrimination was there under the Unionist regime, 1921–1968?', in Tom Gallagher and James O'Connell (eds), *Contemporary Irish Studies* (Manchester, 1983), 1–35; *Fermanagh Herald*, 6 Nov. 1971.

[13] Guy Beiner, *Forgetful remembrance: social forgetting and vernacular historiography of a rebellion in Ulster* (Oxford, 2018), 30; Joseph McKiernan, *By Claddagh's banks: a history of Swanlinbar and district from earliest times* (privately published, 2000), 84.

Passenger, the bus conductor and driver (from the Carlingford bus) walking across a spiked road (1958), *Belfast Telegraph*.

'Not an inch'

Northern Ireland staking its claim before the Boundary Commission

TIMOTHY G. McMAHON

On 29 January 1926 Sir James Craig stood amid what the *Belfast Telegraph* called a 'storm of cheering' at the luncheon following the UUC's annual meeting. The event came less than eight weeks after Craig had signed a tripartite agreement with Stanley Baldwin, prime minister of the United Kingdom, and William Cosgrave, president of the Irish Free State, preserving the geographic integrity of Northern Ireland as constituted in the Government of Ireland Act of 1920. Major Sir Charles Falls, MP for Fermanagh and Tyrone, lauded Craig, saying that his loyalist constituents had 'passed through very trying times of danger and anxiety' without fear because 'they knew they could trust him, and

Irish Boundary Commission's first sitting in Ireland (9 Dec. 1924), HOG88.

they were satisfied their trust was justified'.[1] The heightened
emotions Falls cited among unionists were felt in reverse
among northern nationalists in the four years leading up to
that moment. Indeed, towards the end of 1925, Tyrone and
Fermanagh nationalists were more likely to feel confusion and
a sense of betrayal, such that the Sinn Féiner Cahir Healy
wrote on the eve of the agreement that his community had
been 'sold into political servitude for all time'.[2]

At the heart of this contrast lay the work of the Irish Boundary Commission,
one of the legacies of the articles of agreement for a treaty between Great
Britain and Ireland in December 1921. The treaty had been the product of
months of negotiation between representatives of the revolutionary Sinn Féin
government in Dublin and David Lloyd George's coalition government in
London, the latter having also overseen the creation of Northern Ireland only
months before. British negotiators countered the claims of the Dublin
delegates to the essential unity of the island of Ireland with a defence of the
new state, recognising, however, that some within its jurisdiction might prefer
to reside in what was to become the Irish Free State. Ultimately Article 12 of
the treaty declared that if, within a month of the Free State constitution
becoming operative, the Belfast government rejected Dublin's claim that its
powers extended north, then a boundary commission would 'determine in
accordance with the wishes of the inhabitants, so far as may be compatible
with economic and geographic conditions, the boundaries between Northern
Ireland and the rest of Ireland', and that 'the boundary of Northern Ireland
shall be such as may be determined by such Commission'.[3] The commission
would consist of one nominee each from the Free State, Northern Ireland
and Britain, with the British nominee serving as chair.

Article 12 hung like the sword of Damocles over the unionist community
until 1925. Both houses of the Northern parliament rejected the Free State's
claims immediately in December 1922, and the cabinet steadfastly refused to
cooperate with calls for the commission to begin its work. The integrity of
Northern Ireland was of paramount concern to unionist leaders for three
reasons. First, in spite of the treaty, Ireland remained in an unsettled
condition. Violence in Belfast, as well as along the border, continued into
1922, experiencing new energy because the nascent Free State government
encouraged the northern IRA, cooperating with anti-treaty elements in the
southern counties, to disrupt the border areas, and because the northern

government instituted the USC to augment its security forces. Violence, especially in border towns, included sectarian attacks carried out by civilians.[4]

Second, the decision made in drafting the Government of Ireland Act to include only six of Ulster's nine counties in Northern Ireland had been controversial, not only in the three excluded counties. The UUC, at the urging of Sir Edward Carson, had voted to accept the six-county option in March 1920, but nine-county advocates challenged the result, forcing a second vote in May, in which the six-county option was carried again by a three-to-one margin. Although unionists in Counties Cavan, Donegal and Monaghan led the campaign for a second vote, they received significant support from residents of the six counties, making it clear that the redefinition of unionism from an island-wide community to a six-county dispensation was still an unfinished process at the new state's foundation.[5] Anything which unsettled that threatened its very existence.

Third, in the context of the post-Versailles era – when boundary commissions redrew borders on the continent – recognition that such an eventuality could befall Northern Ireland worried unionist leaders. The conviction of the Dublin delegates that counties with nationalist majorities – and potentially smaller areas with nationalist majorities contiguous with the 26-county entity – should be joined to the Free State exacerbated these concerns.[6]

Long before the ink had dried on the treaty, Craig raised doubts about wholesale transfers of territory. As early as July 1921, he relayed a message to Lloyd George's representative in Dublin Castle, Alfred (Andy) Cope, that he was 'going to sit on Ulster like a rock, we are content with what we've got'.[7] Belfast played a long game, refusing to negotiate meaningfully about transferring territory and slowing efforts to bring Article 12 into effect, despite Free State miscalculations that Craig would eventually cooperate.[8] Craig's actions varied: he participated in the so-called Craig–Collins pacts in early 1922, ineffective though these were on a range of issues including security, returning expelled shipyard workers and shifting territory; he refused to nominate a commissioner throughout 1923 and 1924; and he threatened to resign as prime minister and assume leadership of the people 'to defend any territory which we may consider has been unfairly transferred from under Ulster, Great Britain, and the flag of our Empire'.[9]

Instability in the three regions and uncertainty over the commission's procedures and powers also slowed the process. The Free State remained in a condition of civil war until May 1923 and the United Kingdom experienced four changes of government between October 1922 and November 1924, beginning with the breakdown of Lloyd George's coalition and featuring the first minority Labour government under Ramsay MacDonald. In an effort to demonstrate its capacity, the Free State was the first of the three governments to name its commissioner, Professor Eoin MacNeill, an Antrim-born Catholic and a leading advocate of the Gaelic Revival. During its brief tenure in office, the Labour government pressed ahead, holding inconclusive meetings with Cosgrave and Craig and eventually appointing Justice Richard Feetham of South Africa as chair. When Belfast again refused to appoint a commissioner, the MacDonald administration passed legislation enabling London to nominate on Belfast's behalf. They selected the unionist lawyer and journalist J.R. Fisher, whom Lady Craig referred to privately as 'a most excellent choice, as he will have our interests absolutely at heart, and be as firm as a rock'.[10]

For 13 months the commission gathered tens of thousands of pages of data and nearly 600 submissions from local committees and private individuals. Commissioners toured the border in December 1924 and held meetings across Northern Ireland into the summer of 1925, interviewing witnesses about their written submissions. The Free State, through its North East Boundary Bureau, and the Northern Ireland cabinet, with the help of the UUC, shaped witness testimony. Nationalist advisors, including the Newry solicitor J. Henry Collins, corresponded with witnesses pressing for the movement of large swaths of territory into the Free State, while the secretary of the UUC, A. Wilson Hungerford, the cabinet secretary, Wilfrid Spender, and the home secretary, Richard Dawson Bates, advised unionists, even occasionally taking queries directly to Craig for his attention.[11]

The northern government further recognised the heightened passions among border unionists in those heady months. Fearing a return to violence arising from the commission's recommendations, the cabinet halted plans to reduce the size of the USC in late summer 1924; yet Craig also called a parliamentary election for 3 April 1925 with the border as the primary focus of his campaign, the slogan being 'not an inch', his famous declaration of defiance against any loss of territory.[12]

Despite the understandable fear among unionists that the commission might significantly reshape Northern Ireland, several factors worked to reduce this possibility. Critically, Feetham wielded considerable authority as chair over the commission's work. Rather than moving counties wholesale, he favoured rectification of the border – that is, making relatively minor changes to what he saw as a border established in law. MacNeill, meanwhile, took what Cosgrave later dismissed as a 'philosophical' approach to the exercise, such that he was less an advocate for his government and northern nationalists than a judge of the cases submitted. Fisher took a more active stance, ignoring Feetham's insistence the commission's deliberations remain secret. He was, for instance, probably the source for a story about the likely shifts in territory that appeared in the *Morning Post* on 7 November 1925.[13]

This event touched off a storm of criticism in the Free State, not only because it made clear that Feetham's more modest rectification project would be the outcome of the commission's work, but also that the Free State would lose some territory and population to Northern Ireland, just as it would gain some. Such an exchange ran counter to nearly everything expected in the Dáil, and it precipitated MacNeill's resignation from the commission and from the Dáil. It also led to the tripartite talks by which the existing border was left intact in exchange for financial terms that were beneficial to the Cosgrave government. In the course of those negotiations, Baldwin clarified that the *Morning Post* story was not accurate as to the proposed changes, but it did properly indicate that an exchange of territory was to occur. Had the report been issued, the net effect would have been to shorten the border by about 51 miles and to produce greater net gains for the Free State than for Northern Ireland. Nonetheless, one condition of the tripartite talks was that the final report would remain out of public view. Cosgrave declared that he 'hoped the report would be burned or buried as a bigger settlement had been reached beyond any that the Award [*sic*] could achieve'.[14] It would indeed not be available again until 1968.

Cosgrave's desire to turn away from the Boundary Commission's work as quickly as possible has certainly coloured its legacy in the Irish Free State/Republic of Ireland. How should it be viewed in relation to Northern Ireland's foundation? Based on the government's positioning, the commission actually worked well. Even had its recommendations been adopted, Northern Ireland would have lost minimal territory, gained some (especially from east Donegal) and had a modest exchange of population. The sense of being a largely cohesive unit would potentially have been heightened. Taking the crude measure applied throughout the commission's discussions, with Catholics being nationalists and 'other denominations' being unionists, the projected net gain of 'others' after the transfer would have been fewer than 1,400 people, but the projected net out-migration of Catholics would have exceeded 25,000.[15]

NI Cabinet meeting at Cleeve Court Streatley on Thames to discuss
the Boundary Commission (24 Sep. 1924).

The real benefit was likely symbolic. Craig had championed resistance yet
again, such that the government's and unionists' stance toward the threat of
the commission fell in line with the mythos of the Apprentice Boys and the
pre-war UVF. Their unified opposition served the fledgling state, one that his
own community had expressed doubts about as recently as 1920. Now,
however, his supporters within unionism could declare their space secure by
the concession of both their southern neighbour and the government of the
United Kingdom, a prospect viewed far less positively by their nationalist
neighbours. Now its challenges and its definition would take place within
the parameters of Craig's unconceded inches.

FURTHER READING

Cousins, James A., 2020 *Without a dog's chance: the nationalists of Northern
    Ireland and the Irish Boundary Commission, 1920–1925*. Newbridge. Irish
    Academic Press.
Fanning, Ronan, 2013 *Fatal path: British government and Irish revolution,
    1910–1922*. London. Faber and Faber.

Follis, Brian A., 1995 *A state under siege: the establishment of Northern Ireland, 1920–1925*. Oxford. Oxford University Press.

Hand, Geoffrey J. (ed.), 1969 *Report of the Irish Boundary Commission 1925*. Shannon. Irish University Press.

Jones, Thomas (Keith Middlemas, ed.), 1971 *Whitehall diary: vol. iii, Ireland 1918–1925*. London. Oxford University Press.

Magill, Christopher, 2020 *Political conflict in east Ulster, 1920–1922: revolution and reprisal*. Woodbridge. Boydell Press.

Mansergh, Nicholas, 1991 *The unresolved question: the Anglo-Irish settlement and its undoing, 1912–72*. New Haven. Yale University Press.

NOTES

[1] *Belfast Telegraph*, 30 Jan. 1926.

[2] Cahir Healy to editor of the *Irish Independent*, 30 Nov. 1925.

[3] Doc. 214: 'Final text of the Articles of Agreement for a treaty between Great Britain and Ireland as signed', 6 Dec. 1921, in Ronan Fanning, Michael Kennedy, Dermot Keogh and Eunan O'Halpin (eds), *Documents on Irish foreign policy, vol. 1: 1919–1922* (Dublin, 2017), https://www.difp.ie/volume-1/1921/final-text-of-the-articles-of-agreement-for-a-treaty-between-great-britain-and-ireland-as-signed/214/#section-documentpage (accessed 2 Aug. 2021). See also Geoffrey J. Hand (ed.), *Report of the Irish Boundary Commission 1925* (Shannon, 1969), vii–xxii.

[4] Christopher Magill, *Political conflict in east Ulster, 1920–22: revolution and reprisal* (Woodbridge, 2020).

[5] Timothy G. McMahon, '"It doesn't matter what the authors meant": covenanters in conflict, 1916–1920', in N.C. Fleming and James H. Murphy (eds), *Ireland and partition: contexts and consequences* (Clemson, 2021).

[6] Nicholas Mansergh, *The unresolved question: the Anglo-Irish settlement and its undoing, 1912–72* (New Haven, 1991), 221, 230–31.

[7] Ronan Fanning, *Fatal path: British government and Irish revolution, 1910–1922* (London, 2013), 263–4. The intermediary was Mark Sturgis.

[8] James A. Cousins, *Without a dog's chance: the nationalists of Northern Ireland and the Irish Boundary Commission, 1920–1925* (Newbridge, 2020), 231.

[9] Jonathan Bardon, *A history of Ulster* (Belfast, 1992), 468–9.

[10] Typescript from Lady Craigavon's diaries, 1905–40, entry for 31 Oct. 1924 (PRONI, Craigavon papers, D1415/B/38), 574.

[11] For instance, see Spender to Hungerford, 2 Feb. 1925 (PRONI, D1327/24/3); Eamon Phoenix, *Northern nationalism: nationalist politics, partition and the Catholic minority in Northern Ireland, 1890–1940* (Belfast, 1994); Cousins, *Without a dog's chance*.

[12] Brian A. Follis, *A state under siege: the establishment of Northern Ireland, 1920–1925* (Oxford, 1995), 167–70.

[13] Hand, *Report of the Boundary Commission*, xi–xii, xviii. See also St John Ervine, *Craigavon: Ulsterman* (London, 1949), 498–500.

[14] Thomas Jones, *Whitehall diary: vol. iii, Ireland 1918–1925*, Keith Middlemas, ed. (London, 1971), 236–46.

[15] Ibid.

'Lamagan Choice' by Carol Graham (b. 1951).

Courtesy of the Arts Council of Northern Ireland and the artist.
This painting appeared in 'A New Tradition' in the exhibition
Portrait of Northern Ireland: neither an elegy nor a manifesto (2021)

'Watchtower R21. N/W 1' by Donovan Wylie.

Courtesy of the Arts Council of Northern Ireland and the artist.
This work appeared in 'Chronicling Conflict' in the exhibition
Portrait of Northern Ireland: neither an elegy nor a manifesto
(2021)

Goliath Crane, The Shipyard,
Belfast (1988).

BELUM.W2016.20.234 (NMNI),
MARTIN NANGLE

Section II

A century of Northern Irish life

Northern Ireland
The United Kingdom's first example of devolution

GRAHAM WALKER

The first Northern Ireland Cabinet: E.M. Archdale, Sir Dawson Bates,
Lord Londonderry, Sir James Craig, H.M. Pollock, J.M. Andrews.

Northern Ireland between 1921 and 1972 was the first example of devolution in the history of the United Kingdom. Besides the fact that it was a constitutional experiment, the context of political violence and instability in Ireland in general between 1920 and 1923 ensured a difficult birth. The question of how workable the arrangements put in place by the Government of Ireland Act of 1920 would prove to be dominated the early years and highlighted issues that to a considerable extent remain live political concerns today.

The 1920 act envisaged the creation of two devolved parliaments in Ireland, one for the six-county Northern Ireland and the other for the rest of the island, with the Council of Ireland through which both devolved administrations could work together on issues of common concern. It was hoped – naïvely, as it soon turned out – that the two devolved units would merge into one, and that this might in turn be a first step towards an all-round reform of the UK more broadly. This federal thinking, which had infiltrated debate over the Irish question before the First World War, shaped the 1920 act and reflected the views of the chairman of the committee which framed its provisions, Walter Long. If an example of devolution could be achieved in practice between historic foes, it would commend itself to the rest of the UK.

However, the visionary intentions of the 1920 act were to be stillborn. The parliament meant for Dublin stood no chance of being established in the context of the war raging in the south between 1919 and 1921 and in view of the transformation in the public mood reflected in the landslide election victory of the separatist Sinn Féin party in 1918. The Council of Ireland never sat and the Anglo-Irish Treaty of December 1921 brought in a new form of settlement for the 26 counties in the shape of an Irish Free State with dominion status. This left the new political entity of Northern Ireland as the sole outcome of the original project. Instead of being a precursor to the federalising of the UK, Northern Ireland was to take on the character of a constitutional anomaly: a territory with a distinctive legislature, executive and party system, which was still represented in the House of Commons and very much part of broad UK calculations around government expenditure and foreign-policy matters. Northern Ireland thus brought to the fore constitutional conundrums and political dilemmas that had emerged previously out of the prospect of Irish Home Rule proceeding on its own as a separate constitutional measure.

In what way is the Northern Ireland experience of devolution after 1921 significant for students of UK politics? Firstly, as noted, Northern Ireland continued to send MPs to Westminster. There were twelve members, plus one representing the Queen's University constituency – notably short of the number the new entity was entitled to on the basis of population. It was later argued, by the Northern Ireland premier in the 1960s, Terence O'Neill, among others, that the lower number of MPs represented a trade-off for

Northern Ireland possessing its own devolved institutions and powers, and it therefore provided a constitutional precedent to be followed – as, indeed, it was in the case of Scotland shortly after the devolutionary measures at the end of the twentieth century. Prior to that, Northern Ireland's quota of MPs was increased to 17 amidst the political turmoil of the late 1970s, in the absence of devolution and the failure of attempts to restore it after 1972.

In respect of constitutional conventions, there arose after 1921 the question of whether Northern Ireland MPs would be allowed to vote on issues pertaining to the rest of the UK. Given the small number of MPs involved, this did not seem at the time to present a major anomaly and the MPs' voting privileges were not in any way curbed or limited. Indeed, it was seen as part of the bargain reached in the context of Northern Ireland being in a semi-detached political condition from the rest of the UK. Nevertheless, the matter did make political waves in the 1960s, when Harold Wilson's Labour government had a perilously small overall majority and the entirely Ulster Unionist set of MPs voted with the Conservative opposition. The question was a West Belfast one before it became a West Lothian one in the parliamentary dramas of the 1970s and beyond.

The emergence of the issue in the 1960s also brought into the light the gentlemen's agreement reached as early as 1922 that devolved Northern Ireland business would not be discussed at Westminster. This convention inhibited interventions from the centre that might have been justified on the grounds of upholding the spirit of the 1920 act around the fair treatment of all sections of Northern Ireland society. Such was the reluctance of the British political parties to become involved in Irish affairs after partition, self-interest could be said to have trumped the common good of the UK as a polity, while Northern Ireland's devolution experiment was discredited by allegations of discrimination.

Secondly, Northern Ireland's experience highlighted fundamental financial matters which were linked to questions of political choices and priorities with implications for UK devolution more broadly. The Government of Ireland Act, designed for a very different outcome, left Northern Ireland in control of only a number of minor taxes, the major ones such as customs and excise and income tax being reserved to the central exchequer in London, which decided on the new devolved entity's share. Out of both transferred and reserved tax revenues, Northern Ireland was expected both to finance its services and to pay the imperial contribution that had been part of the original Irish Home Rule plans. These terms had been drawn up at a time when the heavy export industries of the Lagan Valley region were flourishing; however, boom gave way to slump in the early 1920s and mass unemployment resulted. The Northern Ireland government thus faced the prospect of having to honour unemployment-insurance claims as well as maintaining the level of other welfare benefits such as health insurance and old-age pensions in line with the rest of the UK. To do so under the constraints it inherited would have led to bankruptcy.

Moreover, Northern Ireland came into being against a backdrop of political turmoil and sectarian violence. Security costs were high and the first Ulster Unionist government elected in May 1921 encountered difficulties with London in trying to meet them. In July 1922 the prime minister, James Craig, and the minister of education, Lord Londonderry, met with the chancellor of the exchequer, Robert Horne, whose reluctance to continue paying for the USC was clear. Horne, according to Craig, said that Glasgow was also in a dangerous condition at this time and that if Sinn Féin 'broke out in that city' the regular police force would be left to deal with it and the government would not recognise any financial claim regarding damage that might be done.[1]

This exchange is significant – firstly, for what it tells us about British government concerns regarding payments to Northern Ireland leading to demands from other parts of the UK for increased spending on services, a theme that was to echo down the years; and secondly, for the way Horne's comments remind us of the continuing social and political impact of the Irish Troubles in parts of Britain and the decidedly Irish nature of sectarian divisions in the west of Scotland in particular. However, Horne's prevarications were less troublesome to the Northern Ireland government than the outright refusal of the Labour government to fund the USC (the supplementary police force set up in 1920) when it was in office during 1923 and 1924. The USC was viewed by the Ulster Unionist government as essential in the circumstances of uncertainty over Northern Ireland's future – uncertainty that had fed off the prospect of the Boundary Commission provision of the Anglo-Irish Treaty.

The Unionist government led by Craig took the view that London was obliged to put the devolved arrangements it had contrived for its own ends onto an even keel. Although there were those in government circles in Belfast who were inclined to regard their relationship with the centre in a federal spirit and who were acutely conscious of London's wish to be rid of troublesome Irish matters of whatever kind, Craig and the bulk of his cabinet were determined to strive for what they viewed as their British citizenship entitlements. Central to this stance was a pragmatic recognition of the need for the UUP to be able to reassure its working-class supporters that they would not be treated unequally relative to their counterparts across the water. This was politically imperative in order to retain the cross-class character of the Ulster Unionist movement, which had been so evident in the campaign against Irish Home Rule and which was regarded as equally vital to ensuring that Northern Ireland would remain part of the UK.

In the event, the Northern Ireland government persuaded London to revisit the devolution financial settlement. An arbitration process set up in 1925 concluded that the imperial contribution should be a final rather than a first charge on the Northern Ireland exchequer. Moreover, agreement was reached to bring Northern Ireland into the UK unemployment-insurance fund. These changes were reinforced by further agreements in 1938 and 1946, which had the effect of shifting the financial basis of Northern Ireland from revenue to expenditure – in other words, it was increasingly reliant on subsidies from the centre to meet needs. The 1925 outcome has indeed been likened to the Barnett formula drawn up in the 1970s by Treasury officials to determine the amount of government spending in each of the four parts of the UK.

Writing in 1950, a former senior civil servant in the Northern Ireland Ministry of Finance remarked that 'the Parliament of Northern Ireland stands on foundations whose supports it has itself gradually knocked away', and claimed that 'Northern Ireland is in many respects converted into a new brand of Crown Colony though it maintains the status and trappings of an independent legislature'.[2] The same civil servant, in a later article on John M. Andrews, Northern Ireland's second prime minister, said that Andrews, on becoming minister of finance in 1938, had obtained 'a blank cheque guarantee against a budget deficit' from the British government.[3] A distinguished scholar of devolution was to comment much later that 'Northern Ireland was created with the forms of tax devolution but the reality of utter dependency'.[4]

Such appraisals of the Northern Ireland experience of devolution have shaped much of the historical analysis of the province and have led to a tendency among scholars to disregard, or marginalise, Northern Ireland as a freakish exception in discussions of devolution more broadly. Many have been persuaded that there has been little of value to learn from the Northern Ireland example. Yet, as the deliberations of the Royal Commission on the Constitution (1968–73) – the Kilbrandon Commission, as it became known

View showing first piece of concrete being deposited under Parliament Building (Mar. 1925).

– made clear, there was much in the Northern Ireland experience, particularly around financial arrangements, that was to have relevance for devolution for Scotland and Wales. The majority recommendation of this commission, that devolved assemblies for both places should be funded by a block grant and be expenditure-based, was influenced by the Stormont (Northern Ireland) precedent.[5]

What Craig and his government insisted on as he adopted a step-by-step policy of alignment with the rest of the UK in the area of welfare benefits and citizenship entitlements was the right of Northern Ireland still to be part of the broader UK pool when it came to the sharing of resources and assistance. Craig argued that Northern Ireland still had the right to be treated in the manner of other parts of the UK that were suffering economically. This, indeed, was the social-insurance aspect of the union highlighted by academics and commentators.

The Northern Ireland case can also be linked to the recent debate in Scotland during the independence referendum when the former Labour prime minister, Gordon Brown, made a telling intervention in the campaign around this very idea of 'pooling and sharing of resources' as the hallmark of a socially progressive union. Critical commentaries about Northern Ireland being a drain on the British public purse rarely bring into the analysis the way the UK has worked as a broad multinational construct to pool, share and redistribute resources to meet social and economic challenges.

In his landmark study of Northern Ireland, *Governing without consensus*, published in 1971, the American political scientist Richard Rose wrote that Stormont could 'draw upon United Kingdom resources to compensate for sub-standard tax revenues, as would any other depressed area of the United Kingdom, whether in Scotland, Lancashire, or the East End of London'; he also pointed out that Stormont's financial aid was less than that given to Scotland and that Northern Ireland's 'beneficial dependence' upon London was not unique.[6]

The Craig governments – and those of his successors through to O'Neill in the 1960s – used the constitutional arrangements unionists had been given primarily to affirm Northern Ireland's place in the union. Hence the emphasis on step by step in relation to social services as a means of minimising the disjunctive effects of devolution – namely, the detachment of Northern Ireland politically from Westminster (despite the 13 MPs) and from the British party system. None of the mainstream British parties – Conservative, Labour or Liberal – organised or stood for election in Northern Ireland. The significance of step by step was indeed heightened in the post-Second World War era, when Northern Ireland shared in the Labour government's welfare-state measures, including family allowances and the establishment of the National Health Service (NHS). The implementation of such measures benefited all sections of Northern Ireland society and further tied Northern Ireland into the UK, even in a period when it was a devolutionary outlier.

Thirdly, the Northern Ireland experience of devolution between 1921 and 1972 underscored the importance of the treatment of minorities. While the experiment in Northern Ireland may have worked sufficiently well to give substance to arguments about the greater degree of accessibility that devolution afforded to the public in respect of their legislators and rulers, it was nonetheless tarnished by discriminatory practices on the part of certain local councils with whose business successive Northern Ireland governments were unwilling to interfere. These practices disadvantaged the Catholic and nationalist minority in respect of housing allocation and employment, although Richard Rose's authoritative study makes clear that such unfairness was not systematic. For instance, he found that in relation to local-authority housing Catholics were a majority of the recipients in half of the areas studied.[7] More recent academic work has also pointed to the impartiality with which the Northern Ireland Housing Trust, set up by the Stormont government at the end of the Second World War, conducted its work.[8] However, Catholic grievances could also focus on matters such as the application of the Civil Authorities (Special Powers) Act, brought in by the Unionist government in the fraught circumstances of 1922 but never repealed, the conduct of the police, and the failure of Unionist governments to give the nationalist community a fair share of public appointments.

When devolution came onto the political agenda for Scotland and Wales in the 1970s, opponents and sceptics often referred to the Northern Ireland precedent as a warning. In Scotland in particular, Irish echoes were heard distinctly when devolution was put to a referendum in 1979. Tam Dalyell, a Labour MP implacably opposed to the measure, wrote at the time that the debate in Scotland was 'haunted by the spectre of Ireland'.[9] Certainly, Irish questions and parallels infiltrated the arguments of both pro- and anti-devolution sides, although in both cases they were employed to warn voters of the dangers of devolution being denied or delivered. On the part of those in favour of devolution, there were veiled references to possible Ulster-style political unrest in the event of Scotland's will being thwarted. On the anti-devolution side, much was made about the one-party dominance and one-issue focus of 50 years of devolution in Northern Ireland. In passing it might be said that, 20-plus years on from when devolution was finally enacted, the dominance of the Scottish National Party and the extent to which all political debate is filtered through the independence question suggest some tentative Scottish parallels with the Stormont years.

The minority theme has continued to have relevance in the new age of devolution. The consociational arrangements put in place by the Good Friday Agreement of 1998 were to ensure that there could be no replay of the majoritarian form of devolution that characterised Northern Ireland between 1921 and 1972. In Scotland, public awareness of minority issues, either of a religious or ethnic kind, has been reflected in the extensive parliamentary and public scrutiny of sectarianism and concern over the position of the Muslim minority. Moreover, attention has begun to be paid to the experience of perhaps the most neglected of minority groups in contemporary Scotland, namely the English.

Lastly, Northern Ireland's pioneering role in devolution history raises the matter of the importance of intergovernmental relations. It can be argued that injustices and unfairness might have been better addressed within a context of Belfast–London cooperation. However, the intergovernmental activity in relation to the 1921–72 period can be characterised as *ad hoc* and overwhelmingly focused on financial issues, as detailed above. There was,

View from south-west corner of the basement
of Parliament Building (June 1925).

indeed, the sense of the London government deciding to 'devolve and forget' where Northern Ireland was concerned. This 'devolve and forget' approach has also been characteristic of successive central governments in the new broader devolution era of the twenty-first century. Scholars and some political figures have criticised the ineffectiveness of the Joint Ministerial Committees set up alongside the devolved structures and have pointed to the lack of coordination and the failure to strike a balance between respecting devolved responsibilities and ensuring the maintenance of commonalities and collective endeavour. Such matters are now part of the debate on the extent to which devolution has brought the future of the union into question.

FURTHER READING

Bew, Paul, Gibbon, Peter and Patterson, Henry, 2002 *Northern Ireland 1921–2001: political forces and social classes*. London. Serif.

Bogdanor, Vernon, 1998 *Devolution in the United Kingdom*. Oxford. Oxford University Press.

Buckland, Patrick, 1980 *James Craig: Lord Craigavon*. Dublin. Gill and Macmillan.

Follis, Bryan A., 1995 *A state under siege: the establishment of Northern Ireland, 1920–1925*. Oxford. Oxford University Press.

Rose, Richard, 1971 *Governing without consensus: an Irish perspective*. London. Faber and Faber.

Torrance, David, 2020 'Parliament and Northern Ireland, 1921–2021', House of Commons Briefing Paper CBP-8884. London. HMSO.

Stormont in the course of erection, main entrance with scaffolding.
PRONI, D1415/D/14

NOTES

[1] James Craig to Wilfrid Spender, 18 July 1922 (PRONI, PM9/4).
[2] *Irish Times*, 19 Apr. and 3 May 1950.
[3] *Belfast Telegraph*, 3 Nov. 1959.
[4] Iain McLean, *What's wrong with the British constitution?* (Oxford, 2012), 164.
[5] *Report of the Royal Commission on the Constitution*, Cmnd 5460 (HMSO, 1973). See for example 175, para. 578.
[6] Richard Rose, *Governing without consensus: an Irish perspective* (London, 1971), 118–19.
[7] Ibid., 293–4.
[8] Marianne Elliott, *Hearthlands: a memoir of the White City housing estate in Belfast* (Belfast, 2018).
[9] Tam Dalyell, *Devolution: the end of Britain?* (London, 1977), 285.

The quiet before the guns came out

RICHARD ROSE

My first contact with Ireland was a 1954 hitchhiking holiday around the island. All was quiet at that time, including the Abbey Theatre, where I walked out on a play that earned a political as well as religious *nihil obstat*. Writing *Politics in England* in the early 1960s made me conscious of the need to qualify a number of generalisations with the statement 'except for Ireland'.[1] This was particularly true of the chapter about legality and legitimacy, which was weak both theoretically and empirically.

RUAIRÍ Ó BLÉINE

Glór Uladh 1893–1943, Coiste Ceantair
Bhéal Feirste (1943).

When I started research in Northern Ireland
in 1965, my aim was to explain why political
institutions that were fully legitimate in
England were only partially legitimate in
Northern Ireland. The failure of the 1956–62
IRA border campaign to mobilise support was
interpreted as the last gasp of violent
republicans. The Unionist prime minister,
Terence O'Neill, believed that economic
modernisation would replace historic
cleavages of nationality and religion with class
politics. O'Neill explained:

> The basic fear of the Protestants in Northern Ireland is that they will be
> outbred by the Roman Catholics. It is as simple as that. It is frightfully hard
> to explain to a Protestant that if you give Roman Catholics a good job and
> a good house, they will live like Protestants, because they will see
> neighbours with cars and television sets.[2]

After getting off the boat in Belfast in 1965, I told people that I wanted to
look at election results and that I understood Northern Ireland had some
interesting ones. This prompted a laugh and a flood of anecdotes. For
example, there was the story of the 1951 UK election in which the West
Belfast seat was won by an anti-partitionist socialist candidate, Jack Beattie,
by a margin of 25 votes. When an English academic said to an Ulster friend,
'Think how exciting it would have been to be one of the 25,' the reply was,
'Think how exciting it would be to have been all of them!' When I repeated
the anecdote to Gerry Fitt, he recalled, 'I remember the wee Protestant at the
count banging his fist on the table and saying, "If only I'd voted another 26
times!"'

I was welcomed with great hospitality by many people who had never met
a political scientist. Most unionist politicians were optimistic about the
future, notwithstanding signs of opposition to O'Neill's contact with Dublin
being mobilised by Ian Paisley. Northern Catholics noted that the hand of
friendship extended to the Irish government in Dublin was not extended to
them. When I met John Hume in 1966, he was active in a credit union,
helping Catholics get loans cheaply rather than go to 'gombeen men' – loan

sharks. Hume asked me what he should do to combat the gerrymandering that prevented the Catholic majority from controlling Londonderry City Council. I suggested that he should win the Stormont seat held by the Catholic who went along with a system designed to keep politics quiet.

A grant from the American Social Science Research Council enabled me to get a perspective on Northern Ireland by going to Stanford University for three months in January 1967. The children went to Disneyland and I sat in my office at Stanford trying to translate modernisation theory into testable hypotheses about the effect of socioeconomic change on political legitimacy. My theory differentiated political systems in terms of popular support and compliance with basic political laws.[3] With a grant from the British Economic and Social Research Council, I conducted Northern Ireland's first social-science sample survey. Protestants strongly supported the Stormont system, while Catholics did not. While each side approved breaking laws to achieve their political aims, they did so in different ways. Protestants showed a readiness to endorse the use of any measures (that is, force) to remain British, while the Catholic minority favoured symbolic illegal actions, fearing that resort to force would result in a bloody defeat.[4]

Less than eight weeks after the final survey interviews were completed in August 1968, the first civil-rights marches started. I was struck by Irish voices singing the American civil-rights song 'We shall overcome'. One of the organisers, Michael Farrell, explained that demonstrators were bound to sing something and, as a Marxist, he did not want traditional republican songs to be sung. Therefore, he handed out song sheets with words sung by protesters led by Martin Luther King.

Demonstrations were called off in January 1969, when Catholic marchers were attacked by police in Londonderry. A snap general election followed in February. Journalists flew in from London and vainly tried to understand what was going on by learning the names of parties and assimilating what they were told was a British political framework. After four years of imbibing Northern Irish politics, I did not make that mistake. The election revealed splits in the unionist ranks. For the first time in a quarter of a century, Terence O'Neill faced a contest in his constituency. O'Neill won with a plurality of the vote, because the majority was split between Ian Paisley and Michael Farrell. John Hume won the seat in the largely Catholic Londonderry (Foyle) constituency. Change accelerated, but not in the direction that Terence O'Neill anticipated, nor that Hume's new Social Democratic and Labour Party (SDLP, formed in 1970) welcomed.

As I had enjoyed playing in a marching band for American high-school football matches, I went to Londonderry on 12 August 1969 to see the parade of the Royal Black Institution commemorating the breaking of the siege of the city in 1690. By the time of my midday arrival, what became known as the Bogside Rising had already begun. Nationalists had built symbolic barricades a few feet high around the streets leading into the Bogside to prevent the incursion of loyalist marchers. The RUC and the B-Specials posted themselves with riot shields a short distance away to prevent the advance of demonstrators into the city centre. Young nationalist men used hurleys to bat stones at the RUC, bouncing them off the ground to make it more difficult for the police to anticipate which direction the stones would come from. Younger boys filled bottles with petrol, turning them into firebombs that were thrown at RUC cars.

I put on my best American accent to talk with demonstrators and the RUC. Although the term 'rising' has overtones of a violent insurrection, participants claimed that their immediate purpose was defensive. Twice in the past year the police had beaten civil-rights demonstrators and they feared a loyalist march might lead to this happening again. The sight of a blue-and-white flag flying from the top of one of the new high-rise flats in the Bogside made me wonder what a United Nations ensign was doing there. On second look, I realised that the flag was the plough and stars of James Connolly's Irish Citizen Army.

I started conversations with RUC men by asking what time they had come on duty. Many had started their day as early as 6 a.m., being brought from a distance to reinforce the local RUC contingent. By evening there was clearly a stalemate. Because the nationalists could go home for tea or to the pub for a break, the demonstration could have gone on all night. I wondered what tired RUC men would do. After dark the police deployed tear-gas in an attempt to disperse the demonstrators. By comparison with the tear-gas I inhaled when the Chicago police threw it at demonstrators at the 1968 Democratic Party convention, this was mild. Nationalist stones were more dangerous threats to bones and eyes. When the RUC began to disperse, the demonstrators did likewise, and the warm, sunny evening ended quietly without the sound of gunshots or ambulances.

The next morning I went into the bookshop of the Association for Promoting Christian Knowledge in search of information that would help me understand what I had witnessed. An answer was offered in a paperback about the Fenians. Before going to the airport I drove the streets of west

Belfast looking for signs of a Fenian rising or of Ulster Volunteers in action. I was a day early. Confrontations the next night went over the top: eight people were killed – six Catholics and two Protestants. The Labour government sent in troops to separate the demonstrators.

When I returned to Belfast the following month, all appeared peaceful, but the marks of trouble were everywhere. I was shown the holes in concrete lamp-posts on the Falls Road made by tracer bullets fired by the RUC. Over lunch a Falls Road priest told me there had been two men with revolvers on the roof of the parish hall trying to hold off a loyalist mob for hours until heavier firepower could be brought up from the south of Ireland. Elsewhere in the city, guns pressed into use by Catholic defenders were so rusty that the ammunition clips could only be hammered in with difficulty. The bottom line was 'never again'. I went from the Falls Road to lunch at Stormont with Terence O'Neill's political secretary, Kenneth Bloomfield. He introduced me as someone researching the Northern Ireland problem to Phelim O'Neill, a liberal unionist cousin of Terence O'Neill. In his best Oxford manner, O'Neill said, 'I hope you have a treble first' (that is, an extraordinarily good degree).

Although I could see events moving toward violent conflict when writing *Governing without consensus*, it was unclear when, how or even whether a civil war would break out. Therefore, I selected photographs for the book that spoke for themselves. The front cover showed the British army in action in west Belfast. The Stormont parliament building in its parkland setting was juxtaposed with houses that had been burnt out in west Belfast. The next two pages showed the handwriting on the wall: slogans reading 'Up the IRA', 'UVF Here' and 'No Surrender Forever'. The last photo was of the morning after in Belfast: a man sweeping up rubble in front of terraced houses flying black flags of mourning. When my book came out in September 1971, a month after internment, more black flags were on display. The silence was broken and the euphemistically named 'Troubles' had begun.

Reducing the cause of the Northern Ireland problem to economics offered British politicians a far easier solution than my diagnosis of a political conflict involving irreconcilable territorial demands based on nationality and religion. The Labour government was much readier to boost public expenditure than to introduce effective anti-discrimination measures. For example, its terms of reference for the review of Northern Ireland local government under Patrick Macrory (published 1970) excluded any consideration of changes in the electoral system. This meant it could not address the demands of civil-rights activists to end the gerrymandering that discriminated against Catholic

Lambeg drums, drumming contest (1962), *Belfast Telegraph*.
HOYFM.BT.1316 © NATIONAL MUSEUMS NI, COLLECTION ULSTER FOLK MUSEUM

majorities in a minority of local government districts. The Conservative government which came into office in 1970 likewise preferred an economic analysis. When David Howell, a Northern Ireland Office minister, asked me about his theory that most Northern Irish people were moderates, with only a small number at each extreme, I told him that my survey evidence showed the opposite – a U-shaped distribution with most people at the extremes. Howell changed the subject.

Successive inquiries into violence, starting with that led by a liberal English judge, Sir Leslie Scarman, were too little, too late. When I told Scarman that the protection of civil rights in Northern Ireland compared unfavourably with Mississippi, Scarman responded, 'Surely, Richard, you can't mean that.' I replied, 'How about the suspension of *habeas corpus*?' That stopped that conversation. It took the British government 38 years to admit that the death of 14 Catholics on Bloody Sunday 1972 was the fault of the British army, not republican violence.[5]

NILP politicians had repeatedly tried to turn politics into an economic debate uniting the interests of badly housed and poorly paid Protestants and Catholics. Paddy Devlin, interned in his youth because of republican activities, vehemently rejected nationalism, telling a republican critic, 'F*** off back to the 14th century.'[6] The NILP's commitment to the British constitution made it unacceptable to Catholic socialists, who were green as well as red.

The Communist Party of Northern Ireland was so committed to economic determinism that it opposed civil-rights demonstrations on the grounds that they distracted attention from the class struggle. At a meeting I attended, which was addressed by V.K. Krishna Menon, an internationally prominent left-wing Indian, I met a printer who told me he voted Communist. When I asked whether there were two Communist Parties in Northern Ireland, one for Protestants and one for Catholics, his answer was, 'I wouldn't know; I'm from east Belfast.' When I left the meeting with lawyer friends to go drinking at a republican shebeen in west Belfast, one muttered, 'Bloody Protestants.' Not long afterwards, I met a trade-union official from east Belfast who looked to Moscow for a different reason: guns. He explained that the Kremlin was the only certain source of opposition to the Vatican.

At a talk that I gave at Harvard in March 1972, internationally known scholars such as Daniel Bell, Karl Deutsch and Seymour Martin Lipset argued that Northern Ireland's problems were due to belated modernisation and that economic development should end the strife. My retort was that it all depended on what you meant by modernisation.[7] If the definition was economic, then Britain was the first modern country and Marx was its first serious theorist. However, if modernisation was about cultural transformation, then Enlightenment France was the first modern country and Voltaire was its exponent.[8]

At the all-party conference at Darlington in 1972, William Whitelaw, the British government's secretary of state for Northern Ireland, referred to the difficulties of finding a final solution. When Whitelaw realised what the phrase meant in a German context, he corrected himself and he spoke about finding the 'ingredients of a solution'. When I asked Whitelaw to say in his own words what the problem was, he smiled and remained silent. We both knew the problem: there was no solution, at least none that would be seen as normal in Westminster.

At the start of my research I had no firm expectation about whether the economic and social changes under way in Northern Ireland would produce

Uimh. 25. Uim. 1.   mí eanair, 1948   Luac 3p.

RUAIRÍ Ó BLÉINE

113

An tUltach (1924–2018),
monthly journal of
Comhaltas for province of
Ulster.

political legitimacy. When the guns came out in 1969, that answered the question. I continued doing research for 16 years with a different question in mind: what will take killing out of politics and restore order? Publicly and privately I put forward an answer: a concurring majority accepted by both sides.[9] When the Good Friday Agreement of 1998 institutionalised this principle, it confirmed my starting point. The principles of English democracy work well – except for Ireland.

FURTHER READING

Rose, Richard, 2021 *How sick is British democracy? A clinical analysis*. Cham. Palgrave.
Rose, Richard, 2013 *Learning about politics in time and space*. Colchester. ECPR Press.
Rose, Richard, 1971 *Governing without consensus: an Irish perspective*. London. Faber and Faber.
Rose, Richard, 1969 'Dynamic tendencies in the authority of regimes', *World Politics*, vol. 21, no. 4, 612–28.
Rose, Richard and McAllister, Ian, 1983 'Can political conflict be resolved by social change? Northern Ireland as a test case', *Journal of Conflict Resolution*, vol. 27, no. 3, 533–57.
Rose, Richard, McAllister, Ian and Mair, Peter, 1978 *Is there a concurring majority about Northern Ireland?* Glasgow. University of Strathclyde.

NOTES

1 Richard Rose, *Politics in England: an interpretation* (Boston, 1964).
2 Cited in Richard Rose, *Governing without consensus: an Irish perspective* (London, 1971), 301.
3 Richard Rose, 'Dynamic tendencies in the authority of regimes', *World Politics*, vol. 21, no. 4 (1969), 612–28.
4 Richard Rose, *Learning about politics in time and space* (Colchester, 2013), 10.
5 Rose, Richard, *How sick is British democracy? A clinical analysis* (Cham, 2021), 125ff.
6 Rose, Learning about politics, 114.
7 Richard Rose and Ian McAllister, 'Can political conflict be resolved by social change?', *Journal of Conflict Research*, vol. 27, no. 3 (1983), 533–57.
8 Rose, *Governing without consensus*, 551, n. 10.
9 Richard Rose, Ian McAllister and Peter Mair, *Is there a concurring majority about Northern Ireland?* (Glasgow, 1978).

View of army in Ardoyne in the aftermath of a car bomb
(1978).

Orange, green and in the red?
A century of the Northern Ireland economy

GRAHAM BROWNLOW

Northern Ireland's long-term economic performance has been uneven.[1] The record of regional industrial policy in offsetting this unevenness has been at best mixed.[2] This chapter will argue that the most convincing explanations for this unevenness are ones that are not derived solely from economic statistics in which politics were irrelevant; nor can the Troubles, or political instability more generally, be blamed for all the observed failings. Political considerations were responsible for the delay in release of Isles and Cuthbert's pioneering *An economic survey of Northern Ireland* (1957).

Two men on the quayside at the Harland & Wolff shipyard in Belfast, *Picture Post* (25 June 1955).

(BERT HARDY/STRINGER) GETTY IMAGES

Moreover, violence undoubtedly reduced investment levels and additionally created an economy more reliant on fiscal transfers from Whitehall than would otherwise have been the case. Yet some of the most important persistent economic problems, such as underlying productivity woes, preceded the outbreak of violence and have persisted in the two decades since the Good Friday Agreement.

The fact that economic problems, particularly those related to productivity, have proved enduring derives from the fact that three overlapping sources of weakness have existed. First, as part of the UK, the region has shared in macroeconomic failings. The UK's well-documented macroeconomic underperformance has had negative repercussions for Northern Ireland. Second, some weaknesses have represented magnifications of British economic problems. For instance, regional unemployment problems, even during the so-called golden age of economic growth (c. 1945–73), were persistently more severe. The third source is those weaknesses that have been unique to Northern Ireland.[3] The economic challenges associated with the direct costs of civil unrest and its legacy, and the ongoing economic complications associated with the border and Brexit, are some obvious examples. Further adding to the complexity is the fact that the relative importance of these three sources of economic weakness has ebbed and flowed over time.

Given the existence of these three categories – as well as the ways they interact – it is understandable that policymakers have sometimes misdiagnosed the problems or, even having identified the correct source(s) of economic malaise, found it difficult to provide the correct medicine. For example, given the scale of the combined supply-side (structural) and demand-side shocks that the devolved government faced during the inter-war period, it was understandable that their limited policy tools were inadequate to the formidable task. Before 1945 the relatively small scale of regional industrial policy, when combined with the distortions caused by lobbying that tended to reduce its effectiveness, hamstrung any successful restructuring effort.

Less charitably, official reports since the 1950s contained then-fashionable diagnoses of the region's failings (such as peripherality, staple over-commitment or uncompetitiveness) that missed out on important explanatory features related to the institutional environment. Economists and economic historians have long been interested in the interaction between institutional structures and economic behaviour. Analytic narratives of this type abound in the pages of the leading academic outlets.[4] The analytical approach is as useful for reinterpreting the economic record of Northern Ireland as it is for reinterpreting other experiences. The remainder of this chapter will highlight the value of focusing on institutional design in interpreting the long-run economic experience.

That the old staples of linen and shipbuilding, after a temporary reprieve with rearmament and war, would experience a secular decline was largely to be expected in the post-war era. Furthermore, as elsewhere in the developed world, industrial decline has been a long-term feature of the economy since 1945. Manufacturing employment in Northern Ireland declined from 207,000 in 1949 to 193,000 in 1966, 101,000 in 2000 and 85,000 in 2019.[5] The balance between the inflows and outflows from the pool of unemployment determines the level – hence, additional inflows into the pool due to manufacturing job losses were unavoidable in large part. Where devolved industrial policy could be faulted was its failure to generate sufficient new ventures of high quality, which would have promoted outflows. It is macroeconomic policy failings and secular processes of staple decline, which were out of Stormont's control and shared by other industrial economies, that better explain the inflows.

This failure to sufficiently restructure the economy was in turn related to design weaknesses in some institutions within the devolved settlement. In the 1950s and 1960s contemporary academic commentators claimed that the

One of the first DeLorean cars to roll off the production line.
Belfast Telegraph

devolution of regional industrial policy – with its associated ease of access to policymakers – was a competitive advantage for Northern Ireland. However, more recent research paints a markedly different picture.[6] Concerning the allocation of public funds under devolution, the institutional machinery ensured that the disbursement of grants was subject to minimal oversight. Linen was well connected politically and managed to secure large proportion of funding earmarked notionally for the new industries. Likewise, inward investment did not always imply an optimal approach to restructuring. The DeLorean debacle provides a case study in poor oversight and lost opportunities. More generally, an excessively high proportion of the inward investment attracted was often unfortunately of the 'screwdriver' type, with outputs being those coming to the end of their product cycle.

Combined with the large overlap between business and political elites, substantial conflicts of interest existed. This institutional aspect explains why quantitative analysis supports the hypothesis that resources (such as subsidies and advance factories) sometimes went to those enterprises that were better politically connected rather than the ones offering the best private or social returns. The empirical evidence also implies that there were possible opportunity costs – in terms of underinvestment in other areas of government expenditure – of this policy focus. In 1963, when the regulations changed (that is, the rules concerning conflicts of interest were brought into line with Britain's), quantitative analysis demonstrates that this new regime was associated with better outcomes. The emergence of the Troubles ensured that unfortunately the window of opportunity created by this updated and improved institutional settlement would prove short-lived.

In comparative terms, until the mid-1990s, living standards in Northern Ireland consistently exceeded those of its southern neighbour. There is evidence that, on some measures, particularly those associated with income per head, the relative performance has shifted more recently in favour of the Republic of Ireland. Yet, on other relevant measures, such as total (public and private) consumption per head, Northern Ireland remained ahead well into the 2010s.[7] Cross-border comparisons should not hide the fact that by the 2010s the Belfast–Dublin economic corridor represented a population magnet that straddled both sides of the border.[8]

Furthermore, and importantly in constructing any counterfactual histories for Northern Ireland, independent Ireland's economic transformation was not an inevitable consequence of political independence; nor was it unusual in a comparative sense. The long-run growth performance between the 1920s and 2000s does not appear out of line with what its relatively high income per head in the 1920s would have predicted.[9] Kevin O'Rourke notes the similarity of growth performance between 1954 and 1973, for instance, relative to Wales and Northern Ireland. The empirics marshalled by O'Rourke demonstrate a slow transition away from reliance on UK exports. Key to this delayed success was the decision in the 1970s to shift away from the slowly growing UK economy. By participating in the European integration process a new, more outward-looking, diversified and dynamic economic model emerged. His analysis demonstrates that it was only an institutional settlement featuring the policy autonomy provided by political independence when combined with the policy harmonisation afforded by European Union membership that allowed for a superior economic model to emerge gradually. O'Rourke suggests that it was the single-market programme that started in the late 1980s that was essential to Ireland finally reaping the full economic rewards of political independence.

Yet below the headline figures there remain spatial and sectoral fragilities. These fragilities are of relevance in better understanding Northern Irish economic performance. Some fragilities originated before the financial crisis of 2007–8 and have continued into the 2020s. For instance, Irish unemployment levels have not been reduced by being able to ignore fiscal rectitude to the same extent as with Northern Ireland's far softer budgetary settlement. It has also been noted that Irish high-tech sectors (pharma/bio-pharma, medical devices and software) have stimulated exports that have driven the positive income figures. Yet these cutting-edge sectors have not fostered the even spread of local entrepreneurial firms, nor have these firms been able to develop design capabilities. In short, despite buoyant export earnings, the Republic of Ireland's research-and-development share of national income remains relatively low. It has also been suggested that this poor research-and-development record, along with an overreliance on a few multinational enterprises to do the heavy export lifting, represents an 'innovation deficit' which has done little for the even geographical spread of economic activity.[10]

In the more globalised and post-industrial setting of the 2020s, mere imitation of the policy package that culminated in the Celtic Tiger – such as the role of low corporation tax within overall strategy – might not be prudent for Northern Ireland. An extremely positive and distinctive feature of the economy in the early twenty-first century has been its ability to create clusters of new premium service industries. These clusters include activities such as consulting, FinTech, cyber-security and film and TV production. The creation of these clusters is a testament to the existence of pools of talent needed to produce the likes of *Derry Girls*, *The Fall* and *Game of Thrones*. These clusters offer important insights because it has been suggested that successful ventures are not as footloose as was the case in earlier models of manufacturing-based inward investment. Empirical evidence indicates that once such clusters emerge they can be cultivated through an appropriate institutional framework.[11]

In conclusion, there is room for optimism. While no single silver bullet can solve all the economy's long-standing problems, historical evidence suggests at least three interconnected lessons that arise from an analytic approach. Firstly, Northern Ireland needs more adaptable businesses able to produce the goods and services of the future. This requirement for nimbleness at firm level brings us to the second lesson: lifelong learning by workers forms an important part of ensuring greater adaptability by firms. The unenviable equilibrium of low skills, low productivity and low wages can be broken (as the emergence of new service industries illustrates); it requires fresh thinking about education and training that will anchor innovative firms within the regional economy. A final lesson arises from the importance of institutional design. Opportunism and cronyism have been recurrent features of political economy. Witness the examples of Cyril Lord,[12] the Seenozip episode,[13] the DeLorean debacle[14] and, more recently, the cash-for-ash scandal associated with the Renewable Heat Incentive scheme. If the model of future prosperity is to prove efficient, equitable and sustainable, then much greater attention must be paid to institutional design.

FURTHER READING

Bates, Robert, *et al.*, 1998 *Analytic narratives*. Princeton. Princeton University Press.

Best, Michael, 2018 *How growth really happens: the making of economic miracles through production, governance, and skills*. Princeton. Princeton University Press.

Birnie, Esmond and Hitchens, David, 1999 *Northern Ireland economy: performance, prospects and policy*. Aldershot. Ashgate.

Brownlow, Graham, 2020 'Industrial policy in Northern Ireland: past, present and future', *Economic and Social Review*, vol. 51, no. 3, 407–24.

Brownlow, Graham, 2007 'The causes and consequences of rent-seeking in Northern Ireland, 1945–72', *Economic History Review*, vol. 60, no. 1, 70–96.

FitzGerald, John and Morgenroth, Edgar, 2020 'The Northern Ireland economy: problems and prospects', *Journal of the Statistical and Social Inquiry Society of Ireland*, vol. 49, 64–87.

Isles, Keith and Cuthbert, Norman, 1957 *An economic survey of Northern Ireland*. Belfast. HMSO.

Koyama, Mark, 2010 'Evading the "taint of usury": the usury prohibition as a barrier of entry', *Explorations in Economic History*, vol. 47, no. 4, 420–42.

O'Rourke, Kevin, 2017 'Independent Ireland in comparative perspective', *Irish Economic and Social History*, vol. 44, no. 1, 19–45.

NOTES

1 Esmond Birnie and David Hitchens, *Northern Ireland economy: performance, prospects and policy* (Aldershot, 1999).

2 Graham Brownlow, 'Industrial policy in Northern Ireland: past, present and future', *Economic and Social Review*, vol. 51, no. 3 (autumn 2020), 407–24.

3 Graham Brownlow, 'Back to the failure: an analytic narrative of the DeLorean debacle', *Business History*, vol. 57, no. 1 (Jan. 2015), 155–81.

4 Robert Bates *et al.*, *Analytic narratives* (Princeton, 1998).

5 Brownlow, 'Industrial policy', 411.

6 Graham Brownlow, 'The causes and consequences of rent-seeking in Northern Ireland, 1945–72', *Economic History Review*, vol. 60, no. 1 (Feb. 2007), 70–96.

7 John FitzGerald and Edgar Morgenroth, 'The Northern Ireland economy: problems and prospects', *Journal of the Statistical and Social Inquiry Society of Ireland*, vol. 49 (2020), 64–87.

8 Neale Blair *et al.*, *The Dublin–Belfast economic corridor: current profile, potential for recovery & opportunities for cooperation*, Mar. 2021, https://www.dbec.info/docs/DBEC–Full_Report_2021_03.pdf (accessed 2 Aug. 2021).

9 Kevin O'Rourke, 'Independent Ireland in comparative perspective', *Irish Economic and Social History*, vol. 44, no. 1 (2017), 19–45.

10 Michael Best, *How growth really happens: the making of economic miracles through production, governance, and skills* (Princeton, 2018).

11 Torben Iverson and David Soskice, *Democracy and prosperity: reinventing capitalism through a turbulent century* (Princeton, 2019).

12 Cyril Lord was a flamboyant entrepreneur whose textile company eventually collapsed in the late 1960s; see Shaun Boylan, 'Lord, Cyril', in *Dictionary of Irish Biography*, 2009, https://www.dib.ie/biography/lord-cyril-a4889 (accessed 12 Sep. 2021).

13 The Seenozip episode was a financial regulatory scandal involving a Newry-based producer of invisible zips that occurred in the early 1960s and implicated the unionist MP Patricia McLaughlin.

14 The DeLorean Motor Company was a luxury sports-car manufacturer located in Dunmurry, which collapsed in 1982, after only four years, despite an injection of £77 million of public funds.

Being religious in Northern Ireland
1921–2021

ANDREW R. HOLMES

Religion has always mattered in Northern Ireland. Religious commitment tends to be more intense here than in the rest of the United Kingdom and there is a much greater diversity of denominations than in the Republic of Ireland.

The religious life of the region remains overwhelmingly Christian and organised Christianity remains strong, notwithstanding the growth in recent years of other faiths and the number of people stating that they have no religion. Yet religious belief and practice have received little attention from scholars, especially historians. This state of affairs reflects the lack of scholarly interest in the social and cultural history of Northern Ireland before the late 1960s; it is also a reflection of the tendency to explain away religious commitment by reference to what academics think really matters – in this case, conflicting political aspirations. This view is often based on the assumption that secularisation is inevitable in modern societies, which led the anthropologist Clifford Geertz to claim that '"Religion" is everyone's favorite dependent variable' – always being explained by reference to something else and rarely considered a sufficient explanation by itself.[1] Yet the persistence of religious faith in Northern Ireland is not exceptional in a global context. The collapse of Christendom in western Europe is striking, yet in most other places religion in various forms is flourishing. Given these considerations, can high levels of religious identification and practice in Northern Ireland be explained solely by conflict? Can scholars examine religion, however defined, as an independent variable?

Conflict between Protestant unionists and Catholic nationalists has been obvious and often deadly. The conflict in Northern Ireland is not about

Union Theological College.

GORDON McMULLAN

religion as such, though religious beliefs, practices and institutions have played key roles in defining and organising the 'two communities', even amongst non-churchgoers and non-believers. None of the four main churches – Catholic, Presbyterian, Church of Ireland, Methodist – wanted partition, yet they inevitably mirrored the political ambitions of their communities. Sixty-five per cent of the population of the new state were relieved not to be under Dublin rule. For the first 11 years, before the opening of the Stormont building, the Northern Ireland parliament met in the Presbyterian College, Belfast. Until the 1960s, the Presbyterian Church in Ireland, along with the other Protestant churches, existed in 'cocooned complacency', assuming the legitimacy of the state and the duty of all inhabitants to be loyal citizens.[2] By contrast, the Catholic minority were seen by many within the unionist government as a security problem. The assumption that Catholics were rebels was perpetuated in defiance of the fact that during the Stormont years most remained constitutional nationalists and looked to the Catholic Church for leadership and institutional coherence. As noted by Marianne Elliott, 'For Catholics their religion *was* their political identity.'[3]

There are some differences of emphasis between Protestants and Catholics in how they think about religion, though these should not be exaggerated – in general, Protestants tend to be more interested in theology and ideas, while Catholics incline towards ritual and institutions.[4] Theological opposition to Catholicism has been especially significant for many Protestants. This has been exacerbated by denominational fragmentation amongst Protestants and reinforced by the reticence of Catholics before the 1990s to openly criticise their church. Given this background, much attention has been devoted to Ian Paisley.[5] The formation of the Free Presbyterian Church of Ulster in March

1951 and the Democratic Unionist Party (DUP) in 1971 embodied a connection between anti-Catholicism, born-again Christianity and loyalist politics. By contrast, many claim that Catholics are not bigoted and, as Elliott notes, 'in a purely religious sense they have a point'. Yet 'Catholics *are* obsessed about the political ramifications of Protestantism', especially the Orange Order, and were more likely to be opposed to mixed or integrated education.[6]

As a consequence of the mix of religious and political identities, sectarianism is pervasive and deep rooted. A working definition of this phenomenon identifies it as 'a system of attitudes, actions, beliefs, and structures', operating at various levels of human interaction, that 'always involves religion, and typically involves a negative mixing of religion and politics'. It 'arises as a distorted expression of positive, human needs, especially for belonging, identity, and the free expression of difference', and is 'expressed in destructive patterns of relating'.[7] To combat this distortion, the main denominations from the 1960s have sought to create distance between religious and political identities and to grapple with their role as agents of reconciliation. That has not been an easy task and has provoked considerable resistance from within Protestant churches in particular. Though ecumenism has enabled cordial relations amongst the leadership of the main churches, it often remains removed from the lives of many churchgoers. Given the continued segregation of society in Northern Ireland, this remains a major challenge.

No one can doubt that religion typically remains the principal marker of political identity, yet there is obviously more to religious belief and practice. Social scientists of Northern Ireland have demonstrated that there is a weak relationship between political attitudes and strongly held religious beliefs and behaviours.[8] The focus on two communities is understandable, but it does perpetuate unhelpful assumptions and hinders an understanding of the variety and complexity of religious cultures. A survey of churchgoers in Belfast in the early 1990s showed that one of the only things that defined Catholics and Protestants in relation to each other was their perception that the other community was more united and represented the negation of their own political aspirations. Amongst Catholics, the research team found a 'range of theological convictions and attitudes on church affairs and moral and doctrinal teachings' that varied by age and educational attainment. Owing to the proliferation of denominations, the situation was even more complex amongst Protestants. Differences between theological conservatives and liberals were especially noteworthy and, alongside class and age, produced a variety of attitudes to matters of public morality and cross-community relations.[9]

If we can set aside the constitutional question, historically there are a number of religious themes common to Catholics and Protestants that could be usefully explored. The first is religious practice itself, how it was organised and its potential significance. The clergy and religious dominated religious instruction and took a leading role in pastoral work, education and social work, yet there is little research on their collective background, training and effectiveness. Furthermore, we have a general sense about how public worship and private observance were meant to be performed, but what about the actual experience of lay devotion? 'Catholicism provided a great big comfort blanket for its adherents'. Rather than repression, 'most remember a communal togetherness, crowded services, a place to meet friends and a sense of well-being in the dimly lit warmth of the perpetually open chapel'.[10] This was replicated by 'the lively social life within the Protestant Churches'. Because churchgoing was widely accepted, volunteers for Sunday schools and church choirs were plentiful and local churches could support 'a wide range of ancillary activities' for all ages of women, men and children.[11] Indeed, the churches could not have done their job without the mobilisation of the laity, especially women, and the routine work of parishes was augmented by an extensive associational culture. Interdenominational associations brought Protestants together by promoting, for instance, deeper religious commitment and interdenominational evangelism (Keswick at Portstewart and the Faith Mission), student witness (the Student Christian Movement and the Queen's Christian Union) and outreach amongst children and young people (Scripture Union). Catholics had a variety of options, including the Pioneer Total Abstinence Association, the Knights of St Columbanus, the Legion of Mary, and the Sodality of the Holy Name. The importance of routine religious practice for individuals and communities was significant. Its continuation even during the worst years of the Troubles was 'in itself a positive contribution to sanity and goodwill in a time of stress'.[12]

A second theme to be explored is how the churches and ordinary Christians responded to the opportunities and stresses of the modern world. These were exacerbated by economic depression in the 1930s, the Second World War, the coming of the welfare state, 1950s youth culture and the various upheavals of the following decade. All denominations were forced to respond and after 1945 there was institutional and bureaucratic expansion across the board. The Catholic Church erected a significant number of church buildings in the late 1940s; in 1948 the Cistercian monastery at Portglenone was opened and this was followed a year later by a Servite priory in Benburb.[13] After 1945, 40 new Presbyterian congregations were established in Belfast and provincial towns, while traditional Sunday schools and uniformed organisations were augmented by youth clubs and youth fellowships.[14] One of the first expressions of joint action between the Protestant and Catholic clergy was the formation in 1961 of the Churches' Industrial Council in Belfast, which sought to mediate between workers and their employers. A survey conducted around the same time showed that most young people wanted the church not only to preach 'personal salvation', but also to 'concern itself with the problems of our social environment; that the church should, in fact be prepared to lead and not simply follow public opinion'.[15]

Finally, religion in Northern Ireland must be situated in global religious networks. Most churches supported the extension of Christianity throughout the world. Significant financial resources were raised by local parishes and many women and men volunteered for service overseas. In October 1923 the Apostolic Work Society was formed in Belfast to support Catholic missionary activity; three years later a seminary was opened at Dromantine near Newry for the Society of African Missions.[16] After 1945, Protestant missionary agencies gradually refocused their attention from India and China to locations such as Jamaica, Malawi, Nepal and Brazil. In addition to the intrinsic interest of these topics, an examination of missionary activity and how it was supported in Northern Ireland offers an opportunity to contribute to contemporary debates about gender roles and the legacies of colonialism.

The global character of the Catholic Church is underlined by the contribution of two Northern Ireland-based churchmen to the Second Vatican Council: William Conway, archbishop of Armagh, and William Philbin, bishop of Down and Connor. Evangelical networks have been especially important for Protestants. Since the 1950s, this movement, which prioritises individual religious experience and activity, has witnessed a renaissance in the west and a Pentecostal explosion in Africa, South America and parts of Asia. The decline of mainstream Protestant denominations in Northern Ireland in recent years has been offset by a resurgence of evangelical sentiment. It is important to stress the point that, despite the entreaties of Paisley and others, most evangelicals stayed in their denominations. Many treated the national question with relative indifference in comparison to their promotion of spiritual renewal, evangelistic zeal, youth work and social action.[17] Since 1998, the religious faith of many evangelicals has intensified and diversified. The formation of a more directly accountable devolved administration has provided them with an opportunity to safeguard traditional positions on abortion and the definition of marriage, while at the same time highlighting a shared moral sensibility with conservative Catholics.[18]

Christians in Northern Ireland in 2021 continue to navigate the relationship between religion and identity, though the conscious decision of many to do so marks a significant change from 1921, when the division between Protestant unionists and Catholic nationalists was simply accepted. Yet in terms of religious belief and practice, differences within churches have been as important, and at certain times more so, than differences between them. Often the struggle is between liberals and conservatives – however defined – and between those who are open to engaging other Christians (and non-Christians) and those who are not. These issues have become increasingly significant as patterns of religious affiliation change. The number of people who said they had no religion rose from 9 per cent in 1998 to 19 per cent in 2017. Over the same period, regular Mass attendance fell from 81 per cent to 52 per cent; regular attendance at Protestant public worship fell from 52 to 43 per cent. In the context of fitful secularisation, will the conservative turn of recent years weaken or strengthen the churches?[19] On the one hand, those who remain tend to be more committed and likely to share their faith; on the other, declining familiarity with religious idioms offers less common ground on which to meet the non-affiliated and the assertion of conservative views on sexual ethics is as likely to repel as attract potential adherents. Whatever the outcome of these developments, religion in all its variety will likely remain a force to be reckoned with in twenty-first-century Northern Ireland.

FURTHER READING

Elliott, Marianne, 2001 *The Catholics of Ulster: a history*. London. Penguin.
Megahey, Alan, 2000 *The Irish Protestant churches in the twentieth century*. Basingstoke. Macmillan.
Mitchel, Patrick, 2003 *Evangelicalism and national identity in Ulster, 1921–1998*. Oxford. Oxford University Press.
Mitchell, Claire, 2006 *Religion, identity and politics in Northern Ireland: boundaries of belonging and belief*. Aldershot. Ashgate.
Richardson, Norman (ed.), 1998 *A tapestry of beliefs: Christian traditions in Northern Ireland*. Belfast. Blackstaff Press.

NOTES

[1] Cited in B.S. Gregory, 'The other confessional history: on secular bias in the study of religion', *History and Theory*, vol. 45, no. 4 (Dec. 2006), 137.

[2] Patrick Mitchel, *Evangelicalism and national identity in Ulster, 1921–1998* (Oxford, 2003), 231–7.

[3] Marianne Elliott, *The Catholics of Ulster: a history* (London, 2001), 450.

[4] Claire Mitchell, *Religion, identity and politics in Northern Ireland: boundaries of belonging and belief* (Aldershot, 2006), Chapter 5 and 7.

[5] Steve Bruce, *Paisley: religion and politics in Northern Ireland* (Oxford, 2007).

[6] Elliott, *Catholics*, 439, 440.

[7] Joseph Liechty and Cecelia Clegg, *Moving beyond sectarianism: religion, conflict and reconciliation in Northern Ireland* (Blackrock, 2001), 102–3.

[8] Mitchell, *Religion*, Chapter 2.

[9] F.W. Boal, M.C. Keane and D.N. Livingstone, *Them and us? Attitudinal variation among churchgoers in Belfast* (Belfast, 1997), 66, 141.

[10] Elliott, *Catholics*, 470.

[11] D.P. Barritt and C.F. Carter, *The Northern Ireland problem: a study in group relations* (London, 1962), 75.

[12] Eric Gallagher and Stanley Worrall, *Christians in Ulster, 1968–1980* (Oxford, 1982), 125.

[13] Oliver Rafferty, *Catholicism in Ulster 1603–1983: an interpretative history* (London, 1994), 245.

[14] Finlay Holmes, *Our Irish Presbyterian heritage* (2nd ed., Belfast, 1992), 156–8, 163–4.

[15] David Bleakley, *Young Ulster and religion in the sixties: an inquiry into the attitudes to religion of young Ulster people in the 15–20 age group* (Belfast, 1964), 22.

[16] Rafferty, *Catholicism*, 228.

[17] Mitchel, *Evangelicalism*, 9.

[18] Claire Mitchell, 'Northern Irish Protestantism: evangelical vitality and adaptation', in David Goodhew (ed.), *Church growth in Britain: 1980 to the present* (Farnham, 2012), 237–52.

[19] Claire Mitchell, 'Doctrine and decline? Irish churches and the conservative turn', *Slugger O'Toole*, 1 July 2018, https://sluggerotoole.com/2018/07/01/doctrine-and-decline-irish-churches-and-the-conservative-turn/ (accessed 2 Aug. 2021).

Class fractures
Ulster unionism and the challenge of the Protestant working class

CONNAL PARR

Readings of Ulster unionism often fall back on myths and emotive symbols, concealing important distinctions of social class. This essay addresses these divisions by focusing on unionism's class tension: the historic (and shifting) electoral support given to the Unionist Party by the Protestant working class in Northern Ireland and its connected relationship with the labour movement. The latter sought to galvanise working-class politics regardless of denomination, threatening the unionist establishment's success.

The initial cross-class appeal of unionism, with workers and bosses joining forces in an apparent Orange machine, was therefore critical in countering not just Irish nationalism but also the growing NILP from 1924 onwards. Individual leaders such as former shipyard worker William Grant (1883–1949) had bridged the gap between the Protestant working class and unionist elites in government. With the decline of such figures and the later liberalising tenure of Terence O'Neill, the rise of the Reverend Ian Paisley and the beginning of the Troubles, the cross-class unionist alliance was sundered.

Even prior to the creation of Northern Ireland, unionism was acutely conscious of the threat posed by the labour movement. In response the Unionist Party began to adopt labour nomenclature to combat it, with the UULA, fronted by the paternalist employer profile of John Miller Andrews, formed to this end by June 1918. This organisation aimed to ensure that Protestant working-class voters stayed loyal to unionism and would resist socialist alternatives. The UUC – a representative body founded around 1905, with 200 members drawn from local unionist associations – co-opted members and the Orange Order sponsored unionist labour candidates in future elections, with the same representation included on the council itself. However, as Graham Walker has noted, unionism at this time 'spoke only for a portion of the working class, and indeed the Protestant working class'.[1] In 1919 the 44-hour strike of predominantly Protestant (and unionist) engineers – which called for a shorter working week of 44 rather than 54 hours – rattled unionism, as did the Irish urban municipal elections of 1920, in which the Irish Labour Party finished in second place overall. Labour also performed impressively in Belfast, where Independent Labour Party members in the city took 12 of 60 council seats. Following this reminder that the Unionist Party was not able to rely on automatic Protestant working-class electoral support, unionist strategists began linking the emerging labour vote with Bolshevism and disloyalty, using unemployed ex-servicemen in political campaigns to sectarian ends. The Orange Order also expanded its working-class dimension. This targeting of the labour movement accelerated after partition in 1921, when the future of Northern Ireland as a devolved UK entity was by no means secure, though, in truth, the urban Protestant vote was never unanimously in the Unionist Party camp.

William Grant personifies the contingent political bond between the Protestant working class and the Unionist Party from the establishment of the first parliament of Northern Ireland to his death in 1949. Not for nothing did Sir Basil Brooke pay tribute to Grant's 'first-hand knowledge of industrial conditions', as a man who became a government minister but was 'always a worker'.[2] Ever-present in the early and later battles against Irish Home Rule and the tumult of the revolutionary era (he had helped to organise the UVF and was wounded by IRA sniper fire), and a founder member of the UULA, the rangy, plain-speaking Grant was a district chairman of the Shipwrights' Society and had also been a reluctant participant in the 1919 strike. He was emblematic of Ulster Protestant workers who viewed their trade-union culture within a British framework. While patriotic, this was rationally located in economic battles won within British industries. Trade unionism was stronger in Belfast than in the rest of Ireland and, even if Grant combined this loyalty with Orange Order avidity, he wore working-class representation quite literally on his sleeve as MP for Duncairn (north Belfast), with requests from poor constituents written on bits of paper bulging from the pockets of his suit.

Grant's departure in 1949 does not in itself explain the erosion of Protestant working-class support for the Unionist Party, but he did represent a particular link and was never replaced in the establishment. Historians have acknowledged his role as minister of health and local government in creating the Northern Ireland Housing Trust[3] and his behaviour in office, advocating for improvement in working-class conditions, showed fellow workers that the Unionist Party, and by extension the union, could – and did – represent their interests. Unionist governments in the 1920s and 1930s made sure social-service provisions like unemployment benefit, health insurance and old-age pensions were kept broadly in line with the rest of the UK (necessitating increasing Westminster subventions) so as not to raise working-class unionist discontent. There is later evidence that, when the British Labour Party began introducing welfare-state measures – including the NHS – after their landslide election victory in 1945, Unionist Party ideologues considered bringing forward devolutionary measures that would enable Northern Ireland to avoid having to implement such socialist measures. Grant was at the forefront of those successfully resisting these moves, championing the British link in the pushback.[4]

After the Second World War the Unionist Party's political relationship with the Protestant working class began to fracture badly. The warning signs appeared in 1945, when the Westminster election saw a sharp increase in the vote for left-wing parties including the NILP, the Commonwealth Labour Party and the Communist Party. Rising unemployment fuelled NILP advances. By 1962 it was able to gain over 25 per cent of the overall Northern Ireland vote (though, as the NILP's vote was concentrated in Belfast and Newtownabbey, this translated into just four seats at Stormont). Labour figures criticised the 'part-time' quality of Unionist Party government,[5] with ministers holding directorships and running large private businesses at the same time as government portfolios. The Unionist Party's classic tactic for dealing with those who questioned its record was either to dismiss such boat-rockers as disloyal or, perhaps more effectively, co-opt them (as they did Harry Midgley (1893–1957)) into its structures.

An older tradition of independent unionism, representing a check from working-class loyalism, also applied populist pressure on the Unionist Party from outside the official tent. Constitutionally immune to charges of disloyalty and usually armed with ferocious gift of the gab, independent unionist MPs such as Tommy Henderson, an MP in Stormont for Shankill from 1929 to 1953, and the controversial John William Nixon, who represented Woodvale from 1929 until 1949, were a reminder to the Unionist Party that it could not take the Protestant working-class vote for granted. Usually alongside the NILP, they landed numerous blows on the unionist government's handling of unemployment and the economy. Ian Paisley's DUP, founded in 1971, initially emulated the populist character of this class-conscious tradition and even had its own founding representative from this stock in the MP for Shankill, Desmond Boal.[6]

As Marc Mulholland explains, unionism 'had traditionally been led by a social elite distant from the rank and file. The leaders had made up for this, however, by paying a populist attention to the opinions, attitudes and

Vote NI Labour Polling Card (1975).

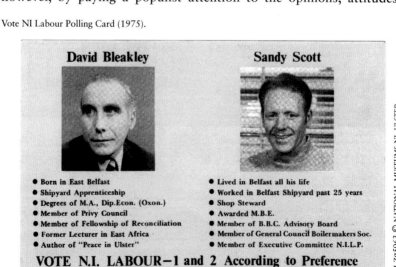

prejudices of their loyalist constituency'.[7] From the beginning, this often manifested in terms of security. Referring to his support for the creation of a reservist special constabulary (what became the all-Protestant USC or B-Specials), Sir Basil Brooke confirmed in a 1920 letter, 'I am not a politician in any sense of the word,' but 'I know what is being thought by the people here.'[8] This *leitmotif* of Brooke's career reflects his instinctive grasp of the unionist base, including a level of sectarian prejudice. Grant was the only minister to survive the changing of the guard when Brooke took over from J.M. Andrews as prime minister of Northern Ireland in 1943. The fresh prime minister and the surviving minister shared strong law-and-order convictions, Orange Order zeal and hostility to the 'priest ridden' society of the south. Brooke's chief purpose in retaining Grant as minister for labour (1943–4) was, however, to maintain Protestant working-class credibility for the Unionist Party government.

By the 1960s Terence O'Neill surfed a developing liberal consensus that believed battles over the border were outdated, winning the leadership of the Unionist Party in 1963 as the candidate best equipped to halt the NILP and co-opt its economic modernising drive. One of O'Neill's chief allies, and a firm supporter of free-market attitudes, was Roy Bradford (1920–1998). Well educated, business-minded and urbane, Bradford was headhunted to advance O'Neill's modernisation programme. The latter urged him specifically to run and stem the rising Labour vote in east Belfast, which he did by winning Belfast Victoria from the NILP in 1965. Other Unionist Party candidates, including Robert Porter, were similarly recruited as individuals of calibre who could advance O'Neill's liberal middle-class consensus, which was designed to move Northern Ireland towards a new non-sectarian dawn of growth and inclusivity – to be presided over by O'Neill's reformed party. This movement attracted liberal middle-class unionists who had stayed outside the Unionist Party because of its traditional Protestant associations, but most working-class liberals remained largely steadfast in the NILP. From the beginning of O'Neill's tenure, therefore, the liberalism of his unionism was entwined with the Protestant middle class.[9] At the same time, Paisley was stirring the Protestant working class.

Having stepped aside as Unionist Party premier, O'Neill perceived in the 1973 Sunningdale Agreement – negotiated by one of his successors, Brian Faulkner – traces of the middle-class moderation he had encouraged. This was about to meet with the final gasp of Protestant working-class power. Usually simplified as a product of paramilitary muscle, the UWC strike of

May 1974 harnessed the industrial backbone that had sustained unionism during the early years of Northern Ireland, with workers at Ballylumford Power Station critical to felling the Sunningdale power-sharing executive (an input absent from a follow-up stoppage three years later, which duly failed). Associated with unionism, the UWC strike was in fact directed as much against those unionists who had presided over the culmination of O'Neill's liberal consensus as against moderate nationalists in the Executive. The Ulster Defence Association (UDA)'s supreme commander, Andy Tyrie, claimed:

> [The strike] wasn't about them [the Social Democratic and Labour Party] being in government, it was about the attitude of the unionist politicians. They never were used to making decisions from partition here. They allowed the civil service to run the place, and it got that bad that we were the lesser-known people within the British government. Our politicians hadn't the sense to realize they weren't important. They were ambushed.[10]

The UWC strike committee – two-thirds trade unionist and one-third paramilitary – rebuffed Paisley's attempts to take over, regarding all unionist politicians, with the exception of Bill Craig and a young Queen's University law lecturer by the name of David Trimble, as duplicitous non-entities.

Instructive are the O'Neillite Unionists who served as Sunningdale ministers, who were all, in different ways, completely scattered by the end. Basil McIvor, Herbert Kirk and John Baxter retired almost immediately from politics to careers in law and accountancy, while Leslie Morrell and Roy Bradford lost their seats in the Northern Ireland Constitutional Convention election the following year. Other O'Neillites had departed even earlier, meaning that the modernising guard, the logical culmination of O'Neillism, had been demolished. On the Rathcoole estate, effigies of Brian Faulkner burned along with effigies of SDLP leaders. Briefly holding all the cards, the Protestant working class handed them back to a new generation of Ulster Unionist politicians after 1974, when further travails lay in store.

Loyalist leaders held some memory of the class divisions discussed in this essay, even if their own class consciousness was so often shaped by the experience of prison during the Troubles. Educated properly for the first time in the huts of Long Kesh and the cells of the Crumlin Road Gaol, such loyalists learned the hard way that Ulster Unionist politicians would rile and ultimately dispense with them when rhetoric was acted on and jail sentences handed down. One of the groups the Protestant working class turned to following the splintering of the Unionist Party was Paisley's DUP, who combined class-conscious distaste for unionism's so-called 'fur-coat brigade' with populist patronage of the Orange machine that served the Unionist Party in the years prior to O'Neill (complete, this time, with a Free Presbyterian overcoat).

The DUP's early class consciousness was not sustained, and unionism continues to fragment, with the Protestant working class now among the groups least likely to vote in any election. In the past decade, the flag protests of 2012 and 2013 and disturbances in 2021 reflect class tensions and unionist communities who feel unrepresented and powerless.

FURTHER READING

Barton, Brian, 1988 *Brookeborough: the making of a prime minister*. Belfast. Institute of Irish Studies, Queen's University Belfast.

Elliott, Marianne, 2018 *Hearthlands: a memoir of the White City housing estate in Belfast*. Belfast. Blackstaff Press.

Morgan, Austen, 1991 *Labour and partition: the Belfast working class, 1905–1923*. London. Pluto Press.

Mulholland, Marc, 2000 *Northern Ireland at the crossroads: Ulster Unionism in the O'Neill years, 1960–69*. Basingstoke. Macmillan.

Nelson, Sarah, 1984 *Ulster's uncertain defenders: Protestant political, paramilitary and community groups and the Northern Ireland conflict*. Belfast. Appletree.

Parr, Connal, 2017 *Inventing the myth: political passions and the Ulster Protestant imagination*. Oxford. Oxford University Press.

Walker, Graham, 2004 *A history of the Ulster Unionist Party: protest, pragmatism and pessimism*. Manchester. Manchester University Press.

NOTES

[1] Graham Walker, *A history of the Ulster Unionist Party: protest, pragmatism and pessimism* (Manchester, 2004), 42–3.

[2] *Irish Times*, 17 Aug. 1949.

[3] Marianne Elliott, *Hearthlands: a memoir of the White City housing estate in Belfast* (Belfast, 2018), 28–30.

[4] Walker, *Ulster Unionist Party*, 64–5, 105.

[5] *Irish Times*, 4 May 1963.

[6] Walker, *Ulster Unionist Party*, 157.

[7] Marc Mulholland, *Northern Ireland at the crossroads: Ulster Unionism in the O'Neill years, 1960–69* (Basingstoke, 2000), 199.

[8] Brian Barton, *Brookeborough: the making of a prime minister* (Belfast, 1988), 58.

[9] Frank Wright, 'Protestant ideology and politics in Ulster', *European Journal of Sociology*, vol. 14, no. 2 (Dec. 1973), 272.

[10] Interview with Andy Tyrie, Dundonald, 9 Aug. 2012.

The Armalite and the ballot box
Republicanism(s) and Northern Ireland

MARGARET SCULL

Republicanism in an Irish context has a complex past. From the IRA, the Irish National Liberation Army (INLA), Official, Provisional, and Real IRA, to Sinn Féin, the SDLP and various other political and militant groups that emerged during the twentieth century alone, approaches as to how to achieve their common aim of a united Ireland have differed in the extreme.

Since the 1916 Easter Rising against British rule, which saw independence declared in Dublin, almost every split and faction of this disparate movement has claimed, at one point or another, to be the rightful heir to this historic moment. It is difficult, therefore, to characterise the republican movement as a single entity. With so many different factions in disagreement about how to achieve the ultimate objective, we might want to consider the term 'republicanism(s)' when referring to the period of the Troubles and beyond.

Following the 1921 Anglo-Irish Treaty and the establishment of the Irish Free State in 1922, considerable violence in the newly created and Westminster-ruled Northern Ireland continued. The IRA attacked the British crown forces, including the fledgling RUC, yet their successes were limited when compared to events in the south. Poor organisation coupled with fears of loyalist retaliation, as volunteers flocked to the USC or B-Specials, hampered their efforts. Small pockets of the IRA were driven underground, where they hoped to lie low and not expose the wider Catholic community to loyalist retaliation.

Although small in number, anti-treaty republican forces continued to attack sites north and south of the border sporadically until 1948. The Republic of Ireland Act, which ended the statutory role of the British

Premises of John Irwin, seed merchants, Garmoyle Street, Belfast, Bloody Friday (21 July 1972).
(MIRRORPIX/CONTRIBUTOR) GETTY IMAGES

monarchy in Dublin affairs, meant the republican movement shifted its focus completely to Northern Ireland. A guerrilla campaign along the border from 1956 to 1962 saw bombings and attacks on RUC barracks. Its eventual failure convinced some IRA leaders to consider political action as an alternative. The movement remained mostly dormant until the civil-rights marches in the late 1960s. As Brian Hanley notes, IRA members acted as guards for the People's Democracy (PD) march from Belfast to Derry in January 1969.[1]

Divisions within the republican movement over the issues of politics and policies intensified throughout 1969 and into 1970, leading to a decisive split. The Official IRA focused on leftist politics combined with armed struggle as the means to their ends, whereas the Provisionals (the 'Provos') were more militarily inclined. Cathal Goulding, chief-of-staff of the IRA and of the Officials after the split, was a Marxist and saw the situation in terms of class struggle.[2] Cumann na mBan, the female auxiliary force of the IRA, supported the Provisionals during the split. By 1972, the Provisionals had overtaken the Officials as the major force in Irish republicanism. However, the introduction of internment without trial by the British government in August 1971, and events on Bloody Sunday, 30 January 1972, ignited a massive recruitment

Girl sitting on a windowsill on Kashmir Road, Clonard, with poster for Irish Republican Army on view.
BELUM.W2016.20.29 (NMNI), MARTIN NANGLE

drive for both arms of the movement. A former IRA member who returned to the movement in this period noted: 'After Bloody Sunday they had complete legitimacy[;] before Bloody Sunday they didn't have any at all.'[3] The spike in membership saw renewed bombing campaigns from both the Official and Provisional IRA. However, community outrage at the Officials' killing of British army soldier and Creggan native Ranger William Best helped lead to a ceasefire in May 1972.

The peace did not last and within two months the battle of Lenadoon erupted in Belfast. Six days of gunfire between the Provisional IRA and the British army left 28 people dead. Back-channel communications between the IRA and the British government also failed and the Provisionals responded on 21 July, when at least 20 bombs exploded in Belfast city centre, killing 9 people and injuring more than 130. The attack resulted in a major public backlash against the Provisionals. Operation Motorman saw British security forces raid republican strongholds and the British army take control of republican areas of Belfast and Derry. Loyalist paramilitaries took their own revenge, carrying out a number of sectarian murders on Catholic civilians.

On the streets, violence increased dramatically. In 1973, the Provisionals began a bombing campaign in England in an attempt to 'bring the war in

Ireland home to the British people'.[4] Arms received from Muammar Gaddafi of the Libyan Arab Republic assisted the Provisionals' campaign. The following year, some elements of the Official IRA, which had respected the ceasefire, grew disillusioned and broke away to form the more military-minded Irish Republican Socialist Party and later the INLA.[5] Vicious feuding between the Officials and the INLA saw key figures from both organisations killed in 1975. By contrast, the Officials publicly proclaimed their intention to fully embrace constitutional politics to achieve their aims. Yet, despite many of their members drifting away to join the Provisionals or the INLA, the Officials were still associated with violent acts until at least the late 1970s. Their political wing, Sinn Féin – the Workers' Party, renamed the Workers' Party in 1982, had minor success in the Republic of Ireland but failed to gain traction in the north.

On 8 February 1975 the Provisionals announced they would pause 'offensive military action' from 6 p.m. the next day. A series of meetings occurred between British representatives and members of the Provisionals over the next six months despite, as Niall Ó Dochartaigh argues, British army anxieties that the Provisional IRA would grow stronger during the ceasefire.[6] This 1975 ceasefire can be seen as a genuine attempt at compromise. Yet, as talks dragged on, it was clear there would be no British army withdrawal

Funeral of Bobby Sands, Milltown Cemetery, Belfast (7 May 1981).
(JACOB SUTTON/CONTRIBUTOR) GETTY IMAGES

from Northern Ireland. Provisional IRA violence gradually resumed as a result, and also led to a change in strategy – members were to prepare for the 'long war'. Republicans were now united in acknowledging that their campaign would likely last many more years and agreed the need for an increased emphasis on the political work of Sinn Féin.

The end of the decade was defined by protests at Long Kesh/Maze and Armagh Prisons. Sparked by the removal of special-category status, many republican prisoners first embarked on a 'blanket' protest and then a 'dirty' or 'no-wash' protest to achieve five demands based on reinstating their privileges. The ultimate protest, a hunger strike, was called first in late 1980, with more than 50 men and women joining but later abandoning their efforts. A new, more coordinated hunger strike began in March 1981, with one male prisoner joining each week. Leading Provisionals member Bobby Sands died after 66 days without food on 5 May 1981. Nine other republican prisoners followed him, as well as more than sixty people who died because of heightened violence outside of the prison.

Republican funerals gained much attention as a result of the hunger strikers receiving almost celebrity status. This in turn presented a propaganda opportunity to the movement. British security forces had often patrolled these funerals and the 1980s saw their presence increase. As a result, the wider Catholic communities began to object to the heavy policing, with individuals unconnected to the republican movement starting to attend vigils, stand outside churches and follow funeral cortèges in an effort to protect the mourners by providing a physical barrier to the police. In turn, these growing gatherings garnered the attention of the press at home and overseas, with Irish America particularly engaged. The striking images, often broadcast on television and printed in newspapers, led many non-Catholic observers and those outside of Northern Ireland to accuse the Irish Catholic Church of being complicit in republican violence by allowing these funerals and shows of republican pageantry to go ahead.

For a moment, the hunger strikes appeared to prove the potential effectiveness of the Armalite and ballot-box approach first formulated by Sinn Féin organiser Danny Morrison in 1981. In terms of the Armalite, Libyan weapons shipments resumed. Sands was among the most prominent of the republicans elected to the British or Irish parliaments, demonstrating the movement's widespread appeal and blunting the arguments of politicians and church leaders claiming the opposite. Some argued the vote for Sands was in the misplaced belief that the British prime minister, Margaret Thatcher,

Memorial to the hunger-
strikers, Derry.

MARGARET SCULL

would back down rather than allow an elected MP to die in this manner. But the 1983 election of Gerry Adams to the Belfast West seat, the first successful Sinn Féin candidate there since the 1950s, could not be explained away. However, political support for Sinn Féin, in both the north and south, was not sustainable – IRA violence was an undermining influence. Constitutional nationalists believed a united Ireland could only be achieved by peaceful means and through majority consent. Sinn Féin lost voters to these nationalists and their political support fluctuated throughout the 1980s.

Republican violence continued, most notably with devastating bomb attacks in Enniskillen in 1987 and on the Shankill Road in 1992. However, behind-the-scenes talks were making some headway. Early discussions in 1987 between Adams and John Hume, the nationalist leader of the SDLP, were facilitated by Fr Alec Reid of Clonard Monastery. These initial talks eventually fizzled out, but communication was resumed in the early 1990s.

On 31 August 1994, the Provisional IRA announced another ceasefire, on the condition that Sinn Féin would be included in proposed peace talks with the British government. Irish American efforts assisted these talks. Loyalist groups announced their own ceasefire in the subsequent weeks and talks finally began in December. However, when these negotiations slowed, the Provisionals returned to violence, bombing London's docklands on 9 February 1996 and Manchester city centre in June. Lured back to the negotiation table, the Provisional IRA again declared a ceasefire in July 1997.

This led to a variety of splinter IRA groups forming in protest and to continue an armed struggle to achieve a united Ireland.

The Belfast or Good Friday Agreement was reached between the British and Irish governments and most of the political parties in Northern Ireland on 10 April 1998. For some republicans, however, several points, such as the lack of any British declaration of intent to withdraw, proved bitter pills to swallow.[7] Radical or 'dissident' republicans did not see the Good Friday Agreement as altering their ideological view and did not believe their comrades died for a power-sharing arrangement within Northern Ireland.[8] The Real IRA splinter group exploded a bomb in Omagh in August 1998, killing 19 people and wounding dozens of others.

Since then, much of the remaining violence has been confined to republican strongholds in parts of Derry and the border counties. Saoradh, a far-left republican party formed in 2016, claims to speak for the true republicanism found in the 1916 proclamation. Perhaps the most infamous attack in the early twenty-first century was the killing of journalist Lyra McKee, who was shot during riots in the Creggan area of Derry in April 2019. Her death saw widespread outrage, with Sinn Féin politicians among the many voices strongly condemning the murder. However, with dissident republican groups using Brexit to strengthen their convictions, the divided Irish republicanism(s) continue.

FURTHER READING

Brady, Evelyn *et al.* (eds), 2011 *In the footsteps of Anne: stories of republican ex-prisoners.* Belfast. Shanway Press.

NOTES

[1] Brian Hanley, '"I ran away"? The IRA and 1969: the evolution of a myth', *Irish Historical Studies*, vol. 38, no. 152 (Nov. 2013), 674.
[2] Richard English, *Armed struggle: the history of the IRA* (paperback ed., London, 2012), 32.
[3] Rogelio Alonso, *The IRA and the armed struggle* (London, 2007), 32.
[4] Gary McGladdery, *The Provisional IRA in England: the bombing campaign, 1973–1997* (Dublin, 2006), 4.
[5] Brian Hanley and Scott Millar, *The lost revolution: the story of the Official IRA and the Workers' Party* (Dublin, 2009), 283.
[6] Niall Ó Dochartaigh, *Deniable contact: back-channel negotiation in Northern Ireland* (Oxford, 2021), 119–45.
[7] Alonso, *The IRA and the armed struggle*, 118.
[8] Marisa McGlinchey, *Unfinished business: the politics of 'dissident' Irish republicanism* (Manchester, 2019), 3.

Troubled love
The north and writing romance across the divide

ALISON GARDEN

When we talk about Northern Irish literature, what springs to mind? An initial thought for many will likely be Nobel prize-winning poet Seamus Heaney. Perhaps you might recall the playwright Brian Friel or novelists Brian Moore, Glenn Patterson and Anna Burns; or Benedict Kiely and Eugene McCabe, both masters of the short story who also wrote exceptional longer pieces. You may think of Anne Devlin or Lucy Caldwell, writers who sing across multiple genres and forms.

Detail from *The marriage of Strongbow and Aoife* by Daniel Maclise.

Across this multivariant literary corpus produced by authors from diverse backgrounds, with differing and often complex relationships to the north, there is a common thread: all have written a variation on the classic story of heterosexual lovers from across the so-called northern divide. Historically known by other terms – the colonial romance or marriage, the national tale, love across the barricades – throughout Irish literary and cultural history, we find writers returning again and again to the narrative of lovers from across the traditional divide to describe the Anglo-Irish relationship or the relationship between the north's perceived two communities. Second only to the thriller in terms of numbers produced, the illicit romance has been one of the defining literary outputs of the north.

This narrative has a much longer history than that of the Northern Irish statelet. Forbidden love has been a staple of Irish culture for centuries. The various cycles of Irish mythology preserved in Old and Middle Irish texts contain the fatal love stories of Deirdre and Naoise, Gráinne and Diarmuid and Tristan and Iseult, amongst others. It is often argued that the marriage of Aoife Mac Murchada, daughter of the Irish chieftain Diarmait Mac Murchada (*c.* 1110–1171), to the Anglo-Norman earl Richard Fitzgilbert de Clare (alias Strongbow), led to the second, much larger and more successful Anglo-Norman invasion of Ireland in the twelfth century. This strategic marriage is, in numerous ways, a vital strand of the Irish national story; or, at least, central to the idea of how 'the "English" gained their foothold in Ireland … [and] 800 years of dispossession and oppression took hold'.[1] Daniel Maclise's monumental painting of this wedding, *The marriage of Strongbow and Aoife* (1854), hangs in pride of place in the Millennium Wing of the National Gallery of Ireland in Dublin.

Maclise's painting is one example of a cultural narrative that has three distinct literary permutations: the colonial romance, the national tale and the 'love across the divide' story. All of these manifestations can be mapped onto and traced back to specific historical moments and all intersect with the particular political contexts of these moments. The colonial romance has its roots in the imperial romance and early colonial discourse of the sixteenth and seventeenth centuries. As early modern European efforts to subjugate the so-called 'New World' intensified in the sixteenth and seventeenth centuries, a cohesive political and cultural discourse was produced to justify this colonial enterprise, which could be applicable closer to home, too.

Echoing ways of writing used by other European imperial powers to describe their would-be colonial territories, Ireland was increasingly envisaged as virgin territory ready for imperial penetration, in need of patriarchal control from her eastern neighbour.

The afterlives of this way of thinking can be found, for example, in Seamus Heaney's controversial poems 'Act of Union' and 'Ocean's love to Ireland', from *North* (1975). Critics have argued that such poems epitomise this rhetoric, with their knowing nods to imperial romances by Walter Raleigh, an 'imperially / Male' England and a violated woman, Ireland.[2] There was an Irish tradition of envisioning Ireland as a woman, too, and such allegorical self-fashioning of the 'motherland' was central to multiple cultural traditions from early pre-Christian mythology, to Irish-language 'aisling' poetry and later nineteenth- and twentieth-century cultural nationalism. Such rhetoric has important consequences for the literary history we are tracing here: it eroticises and feminises Ireland, suggesting 'she' is a romantic partner to Britain.

The suggestion that Ireland was a natural wife to Britain came to fruition with the 1800 Act of Union, which united Ireland and Great Britain into the United Kingdom, and which came into effect in 1801. The Act of Union was famously and 'consistently depicted as a marriage, with … Ireland as the bride' and the culturally pervasive 'metaphor … reappeared not only in cartoons and popular entertainment, but also in parliamentary speeches of the period'.[3] It was also adopted into the literary genre of the national tale, a genre named after Sydney Owenson's novel *The wild Irish girl: a national tale*, from 1806. While the term 'national tale' is, Miranda Burgess cautions, 'slippery, still open to question or argument', in Ireland, national tales were 'centrally concerned with definitions and descriptions of' the 'nation'. These texts often involved a marriage plot, almost exclusively between an Irish Catholic woman and a British, or Anglo-Irish, Protestant man, signalling the union between the two nations and attempting to smooth an uncomfortable, coerced relationship into something more palatable.[4] Despite the tired critical argument that romance is an apolitical genre, these stories of love and marriage did some serious heavy lifting in the post-union cultural landscape.

While the romance across the divide never went away, it proliferated after the partition of the island and again during the period of conflict in the late twentieth-century euphemistically referred to as the Troubles. Whereas the colonial romance, and frequently the national tale, relied on a clear demarcation of Irish and outsider, in the northern take on the trope often –

though not exclusively – both lovers came from within the new, and contentious, statelet. Joe Cleary, one of the few academics to have written about the phenomenon of these types of love stories, declares that the northern 'romance-across-the-divide is an anxious and contradictory literary mode'. These texts, he maintains, are marked by a frustrated effort for lovers from 'antagonistic communities' to come together in romantic union; this 'nationalising embrace', as he terms it, could – but fails to – act as a metaphorical consolidation of the nation state. This union or 'nationalising embrace' can never be achieved in the case of 'Northern Irish' texts because the right of the northern statelet to exist at all is contested.[5] Despite the emotional optimism of the desire between individuals, imagined unions seem impossible in a society shaped by suspicion and division.

Of course, the mention of union and division in Ireland brings up the spectre of partition. Cleary's analysis of twentieth-century Irish fiction, especially novels, makes much of the conspicuous absence of any real engagement with the other side of the border: north and south are dealt with in 'hermetically compartmentalised terms'.[6] In this way partition itself is effaced and the two states, and their ostensibly irreconcilable cultures, are kept apart. But this hypothesis does not always hold when we read some love-across-the-divide narratives carefully. Brian Moore's *The feast of Lupercal* (1958), Dermot Healy's *A goat's song* (1994), Kate O'Riordan's *Involved* (1995) and Lucy Caldwell's *Where they were missed* (2006), for example, have lovers from both sides of the border, as does Jan Carson's playful take on the trope in the title story from *Children's children* (2016). In all of these examples, the border is crossed numerous times; in Carson's story, it is a central aspect of the story's plot.

These love stories are significantly more complex than we might anticipate and often unsettle other binaries or divides. In Eugene McCabe's *Death and nightingales* (1992), there are multiple pairs of 'antagonistic lovers', but a central pair, Beth and Liam, are actually both Catholic, even though Beth has been forbidden from marrying a Catholic by her Protestant stepfather. In Jennifer Johnston's *Shadows on our skin* (1977), a young woman from Wicklow works as a teacher in Derry but is engaged to a British soldier, who is on active duty in Germany. In Bernard MacLaverty's *Cal* (1983), a getaway driver in an IRA assassination of a RUC officer becomes entangled with his widow when it is revealed that her family are actually Italian and Catholic. Neil Jordan's film *The crying game* (1992) sees a former IRA man flee to London and begin a relationship with a woman of colour, involving one particularly revealing scene (in more than one sense of the word) that shocked audiences in a way that we would likely find questionable now.

Arguably the most famous example of these romances is Joan Lingard's series of five young-adult novels about Protestant Sadie and Catholic Kevin, the second of which, *Across the barricades* (1972), was routinely read as part of the school curriculum in the north and also in western Scotland. Adored by readers around the world, Kevin and Sadie flee Belfast for Britain at the end of *Across the barricades* to marry and start a family. The subsequent three novels chart not only the anti-Irish racism that they face as migrants in England and Wales, but also the difficulties of building an intimate life with someone from a different community, in addition to the challenges – and boredom – of domesticity and childrearing. The popularity of the narrative continues; in April 2021, Sue Divin published *Guard your heart* (2021), a love story about Catholic Aiden and Protestant Iona, both born in Derry on 10 April 1998, the day 'The Good Friday Agreement, or Belfast Agreement' was signed.

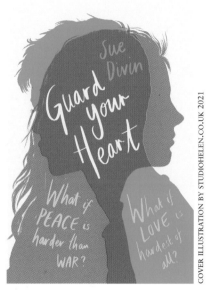

From Guard Your Heart (2021).
MACMILLAN PUBLISHERS INTERNATIONAL LIMITED.

Too often, these stories have suffered for want of engaged readings and have been glossed purely at the level of plot: do the lovers end up together and, if so, where? To dismiss these narratives as indicative of imaginative failure because their romantic plots are frustrated or comprised is to do them a grave disservice. Engaging these narratives through a granular focus that takes them seriously both as works of fiction and as cultural phenomena is profoundly revealing. We ought to read these narratives with an acute eye to their depiction of the everyday and ostensibly mundane, without losing sight of the national narratives, or even stereotypes, with which these stories are in dialogue. These stories do function in multiple ways, even if we cannot view them as a monolith. They give us intimate details about life in a particular place, at a particular time, and the intersectional pressures that are brought to bear upon it. They do this even as they have been used as shorthand to explain Northern Ireland's unique political situation or, more perniciously, to simplify or dehistoricise the conflict of the Troubles. In this way, these love stories have sometimes done fascinating memory work – translating lived experience into romanticised myth – even while the conflict was still unfolding. These love stories are part of the dynamic literary, cultural and political history shared between Britain and Ireland, where the allegedly private worlds of intimacy and desire have been so frequently forced into the public arena. But desire is unruly and these stories reflect this. They depict, but barely contain, the north; where life and love constantly spill beyond the putative 'twin blocs', or the statelet's contentious border.

FURTHER READING

Caldwell, Lucy, 2006 *Where they were missed*. London. Viking Press.
Carson, Jan, 2016 *Children's children*. Dublin. Liberties Press.
Davies, Eli, 2021, 'Remembering the Home and the Northern Irish Troubles', in Oona Frawley ed. *Women and the Decade of Commemorations*. Bloomington: Indiana University Press. pp. 284–99.
Divin, Sue, 2021 *Guard your heart*. London. Pan Macmillan.
Ferris, Ina, 2002 *The romantic national tale and the question of Ireland*. Cambridge. Cambridge University Press.
Healy, Dermot, 1994 *A goat's song*. London. Harvill.
Johnston, Jennifer, 1977 *Shadows on our skin*. London. Hamilton.
Jordan, Neil, 1992. *The crying game*. Miramax.
Kennedy-Andrews, Elmer, 2003 *Fiction and the Northern Ireland Troubles since 1969: (de-)constructing the north*. Dublin. Four Courts Press.
Lingard, Joan, 1972 *Across the barricades*. London. Hamilton.
MacLaverty, Bernard, 1983 *Cal*. Belfast. Blackstaff Press.
Magennis, Caroline, 2021 *Northern Irish writing after the Troubles: intimacies, affects, pleasures*. London. Bloomsbury.
McCabe, Eugene, 1992 *Death and nightingales*. London. Secker and Warburg.
Moore, Brian, 1958 *The feast of Lupercal*. London. André Deutsch.
O'Riordan, Kate, 1995 *Involved*. London. Flamingo.
Wills, Clair, 1993 *Improprieties: politics and sexuality in Northern Irish poetry*. Oxford. Clarendon Press.

NOTES

[1] Gerry Smyth, *The Judas kiss: treason and betrayal in six modern Irish novels* (Manchester, 2015), 3.
[2] Seamus Heaney, 'Act of Union', *North* (London, 1975), 49.
[3] Jane Elizabeth Doughtery, 'Mr and Mrs England: the Act of Union as national marriage', in Dáire Keogh and Kevin Whelan (eds), *Acts of Union: the causes, contexts and consequences of the Act of Union* (Dublin, 2001), 202.
[4] Miranda Burgess, 'The national tale and allied genres', in John Wilson Foster (ed.), *The Cambridge companion to the Irish novel* (Cambridge, 2006), 39.
[5] Joe Cleary, *Literature, partition and the nation state: culture and conflict in Ireland, Israel and Palestine* (Cambridge, 2002), 112, 113, 115.
[6] Cleary, *Literature, partition and the nation state*, 77.

Woman on Royal Avenue (1988), with
Post Office opposite.
BELUM.W2016.20.317 (NMNI), MARTIN NANGLE

Teenage Kicks?
Vignettes of youth culture across Northern Ireland

GARETH MULVENNA

As a relatively modern concept, the emergence of the idea of the teenager in post-war western society heralded a dramatic rise in youth-culture studies among scholars. Despite this, in the hundred years since the formation of Northern Ireland, relatively little emphasis has been placed on understanding youth culture and its place in the making of historical events in the region. An examination of youth culture can assist in a better understanding of some of the most pivotal events in Northern Ireland's centennial history. While it would be all but impossible to cover every aspect of this subject in one chapter, an attempt will be made to focus on specific examples and the way in which they relate to the state of Northern Ireland at the time.

(ORIGINAL CAPTION): Teenagers stand amid the ruins of Smithfield Market in Belfast, wearing parallels, one of the fashionable trouser styles of the '70s.

(HULTON DEUTSCH/CONTRIBUTOR) GETTY IMAGES

The restrictive force of Sabbatarianism pervaded life in Northern Ireland in the first half of the century. In turn, this affected the opportunities for young people to enjoy a fully dynamic social life. The future UVF leader Gusty Spence was born in 1933 and described the typical Sunday routine for teenagers in the greater Shankill area:

> No cinemas or pubs were open on Sundays and the done thing was to walk up the Shankill Road, up the Ballygomartin Road and round the side of the hill, about four miles. There was a big green square there and literally hundreds of young fellows and girls were pairing off and sitting having a yarn or smoking wee butts.

The tedious scenario Spence remembered largely formed around the intransigence of Belfast Corporation, which decreed that Sunday should be a day of observance on which even children's playgrounds were closed: 'we were full of life but Belfast must have been one of the most miserable towns ever'.[1]

Spence painted a grim portrait of an arrested youth culture, but it would not be long before young people became the focus of a moral panic in Ulster. The Teddy Boy subculture has been described as 'the first youth movement of post-war Britain'.[2] Northern Ireland was not immune to the moral panic that accompanied the rise of the Teddy Boy. For such a socially conversative society, the sight of young men in long, draped jackets and tight-fitting trousers was a significant shock to the older generation, who often depended on young people to adopt and nurture the political allegiances of each ethnic bloc. Given the sectarian nature of Belfast's working-class industrial neighbourhoods, it was inevitable that casual violence would act as a microcosm of broader historical conflict. Thus, the Teddy Boy culture in Belfast inflamed sectarian passions so significantly that there was a fear in 1955 that it could cause the complete disintegration of old shibboleths.[3]

Those shibboleths began to collapse to an extent with the advent of the counterculture of the mid to late 1960s. This wind of change captured the imagination of young people in Northern Ireland. In 1963 American singer-songwriter Joan Baez resurrected the old gospel hymn 'We Shall Overcome' during the march on Washington. The song became an anthem of the African American civil-rights movement and 'the most resounding protest anthem in America'. In Northern Ireland Eamonn McCann, a leading activist with the Derry Housing Action Committee (DHAC), was part of a protest against discriminatory housing allocation in the city. McCann recalls that during similar situations previously the crowd would sing '"Kevin Barry" or more likely "The Soldier's Song" or something like that'. On 3 July 1968, as Mayor William Beattie was due to cut the ribbon on the new Craigavon Bridge in Derry, members of the DHAC sat down and blocked the bridge. McCann was at the side with several others, cheering his fellow protestors on: 'At that stage the police arrived and people didn't know what to do. I just stepped forward, singing "We Shall Overcome".'[4]

Some young loyalists were curious about this emerging culture of protest among their nationalist counterparts. Born in 1955, Robert Niblock was from the staunchly loyalist working-class Lagan Village neighbourhood of east Belfast. In 1968 he was attending Annadale Grammar School and remembers his English teacher, Ronnie McNamee, bringing examples of popular culture into the classroom:

> he was the first person I heard talking about equal rights. He incorporated it into some of our classes as he did with his favourite pastime – listening to music. It was quite common for him to play one of his LPs in class, then pick a track and put the lyrics on the board for us to talk about. It was usually something like a Bob Dylan song, Woody Guthrie, Tom Paxton and on one occasion he had us dissecting the lyrics of 'Lucy in the Sky with Diamonds' by The Beatles. Of course we couldn't wait to get home to impress all our mates that we knew this great song which was actually about drugs!![5]

McNamee's audience was mainly Protestant and middle class, but he encouraged discussion among his pupils and sought to accommodate Niblock's views into a classroom debate. McNamee had told his charges that change was occurring throughout the world and that Ireland would follow suit. Niblock remembers his feelings at the time:

> My attitude to this I suppose was predictable. Based on what I had been told and what I believed to be true I told him that the Catholics were only looking something to yap about and anyway they wouldn't dare start anything because they knew what would happen to them if they did.[6]

Niblock was curious about what he had been told. After seeing McNamee with a poster for a PD rally, he decided to go and see for himself who the protestors were. At the protest Niblock encountered members of PD singing 'We Shall Overcome'. There was never any question of his interest in the motivations of the protestors forming an epiphany. Niblock's maternal uncles

(ORIGINAL CAPTION): Youngsters stand outside a record shop hoping to listen to free spins near Smithfield market in Belfast (9 Oct. 1963).

were steeped in the loyalist tradition and ultimately had a more significant influence on his development. He became involved in the loyalist paramilitaries in 1972 as a 17-year-old and is now an accomplished writer.

Despite the widespread support for civil-rights campaigning in the Catholic community, some of the cultural blowbacks of the 1960s did not go down well with the parent generation. Sharon O'Connor from Ardoyne remembers that during the tumultuous and violent summer of 1969 'there was a fashion … for washed-out, almost white jeans, which is very aspirational in a community that didn't have great laundry facilities'. O'Connor recalls how teenagers in her area quickly went from being pariahs to occupying a central position in the community as local adults prepared for communal defence against loyalists:

Teenagers were dismissed then as they are now. Long hair was quite a thing then. My father made everyone get the standard short back and side[s] and strongly disapproved of jeans; he was extremely uncomplimentary of anyone with long hair, as they were judged to be undesirable. This give [*sic*] rise to one of my standout memories, which is my granny saying: 'It was those long-haired louts they talk about. They are the ones who were trying to help.' Suddenly, in her eyes and in reality, these 'useless' teenagers were the defenders and heroes of the hour![7]

Youth subcultures and gangs which would have been identified as a social menace in normal times, such as the Teddy Boys, were now being accommodated and pushed to the forefront of the growing sectarian turmoil. In loyalist communities the phenomenon of the Tartan gangs had accelerated in tandem with the violence and provided ready-made foot soldiers for the loyalist paramilitaries.[8] Writing in *New Society* (July 1972), Sue Jenvey observed that the 'Tartan' and 'Fianna' gangs seem to be an adolescent mirror image of the UDA/UVF and IRA militarism: 'The "normal" hostilities between the older and younger generations are becoming tragically bridged.'[9] In his classic study of youth culture and sectarianism in Northern Ireland, Desmond Bell observed:

> Militant Loyalism is clearly not capable of providing a *political* solution to the material problems confronting Protestant youth … It remains however an important *cultural resource* for the 'new dispossessed' Protestant youth of Northern Ireland, as indeed Republicanism is for Catholic youth.[10]

Different cultural resources came into play for other working-class youths in the mid-1970s with the emergence of punk rock. With its emphasis on DIY fashion and simplistic but effective music, many young people who had grown up during the era of bloated progressive rock saw an opportunity to respond to political events through a creative medium. In October 1976 The Damned, who hailed from London, released what is now regarded as the first UK punk-rock single, 'New Rose'; this was soon followed in November by 'Anarchy in the UK' – a song that would propel fellow Londoners the Sex Pistols to the position of the establishment's number-one *bête noire*. Young people in Northern Ireland could hardly have failed to notice a verse in the song which directly mentioned two of the protagonists in the ongoing violence occurring around them:

Is this the MPLA?
Or is this the UDA?
Or is this the IRA?
I thought it was the UK
Or just another country
Another council tenancy[11]

With a tense atmosphere that was ready made for the arrival of the punk subculture, Northern Ireland would forge its own scene. What is peculiar, however, is that Northern Irish punk, in the main, did not respond directly to what was going on in the country at the time. The scene's biggest export, The Undertones, sang of mainly frivolous things such as girls and Subbuteo. Perhaps that is what young people needed – an escape, an anthem such as 'Teenage Kicks'. Not all of those who lived in working-class areas, where the violence was at its worst, saw the punk scene as a genuine attempt to be inclusive. Indeed, there was a negative attitude toward bands such as Stiff Little Fingers, whom some viewed as cashing in on the image of Belfast as a war-torn news headline. Referring to the success of Stiff Little Fingers, Paul Burgess, drummer and songwriter of Ruefrex, has noted:

> we were very suspicious of it because most of the early hits like Suspect Device … were written by an English journalist called Gordon Ogilvie. That would've been beyond the pale for us[:] it seemed so incongruous and so insulting to have not just a journalist but an English journalist writing these lyrics that were quintessentially about what it was like to be suffering from the Troubles in Northern Ireland.[12]

Despite Burgess's reservations, 'Alternative Ulster' became an anthem for a disaffected youth. With its lyrics including 'Ignore the bores and their laws / Get an alternative Ulster', the song has been adopted by a new generation of young people campaigning for equality and a different society in the Northern Ireland of 2021.

Ruefrex at BBC
studios, Balmoral
(beside King's Hall,
3 Oct. 1983).

ALASTAIR GRAHAM

Although punk is largely considered to have brought young people together, the reality was that Northern Ireland was a sectarian society. Henry McDonald has written of his experiences during the punk era, when he followed Cliftonville Football Club, a team which by the late 1970s had been co-opted by republicans:

> We were, and are, coloured by our roots and background. As already described, between '78 and '81 I lived out a double-life, with loyalties that straddled the Cornmarket punks and the faithful at Solitude, home of Cliftonville.[13]

McDonald has identified 1981 as a 'crucial and arguably fatal' year 'in the history of Ulster punk', with the deaths of protesting republican prisoners on hunger strike in the H-blocks and the emergence on the scene of racist bands such as Offensive Weapon (whose members included future UDA young Turks Johnny Adair and Sam McCrory).[14] The calcification of relations between the two communities once again set in and as the 1980s ground on there was little for young people in Northern Ireland to be joyous about. Thatcherism had a devastating effect on society, with youth unemployment rising, glue-sniffing and drug abuse spiralling out of control and the Troubles settling into a long-war phase.

As the secretly nourished seeds of a peace process began to flower in the early 1990s, violence on the streets increased. Paramilitaries, particularly those former young punks from Offensive Weapon, decided to accelerate and intensify the bloodletting in the hope of weakening the Provisional IRA/Sinn Féin paramilitary and political machine. On the cusp of this era, in the winter of 1989–90, a young mod from the Ormeau Road by the name of David Holmes was working as hairdresser. He decided to start a club night with his colleague Iain McCready. The venue was the Art College; the club's name was Sugar Sweet. Writing for *The Guardian* on the occasion of the thirtieth anniversary of Sugar Sweet, Holmes recalled:

> Everything was so fresh and raw. All week you're getting searched, there's roadblocks, it takes three hours to get home – people are being shot on your fucking doorstep. But when you're living in that moment, you don't feel that you're being affected by it. If you spend Monday to Saturday living in fear and paranoia, once you cross into that club and you're hearing this music from all over the world, while being psychedelically intoxicated, all that shit just disappears … There was all this energy released. These communities fucking hated each other but among them you had groups of people whose religion was music.[15]

Sugar Sweet

The legacy of Sugar Sweet cannot be overstated. It brought young people together during a crucial phase of the conflict that saw a gradual transition from all-out war to peaceful dialogue. Many of the friendships created at the club endured and that spirit of coexistence successfully bled into the creation of a more liberal, outward-looking generation whose presence can be strongly felt on the margins of the current political arena.

Throughout the history of Northern Ireland youth culture has provided a vehicle for young people to cross the sectarian divide, but it has also been at the epicentre of some of the most memorable incidents of sectarian division and violence. Youth culture does not exist in a vacuum and the external forces and pressures of life in a divided society often came to bear on how young people in Northern Ireland expressed their identities.

FURTHER READING

Bailie, Stuart, 2018 *Trouble songs: music and conflict in Northern Ireland*. Belfast. Bloomfield.

Bell, Desmond, 1990 *Acts of union: youth culture and sectarianism in Northern Ireland*. Basingstoke. Macmillan.

Darby, John and Morris, Geoffrey, 1974 *Intimidation in housing*. Belfast. Community Relations Commission.

Garland, Roy, 2001 *Gusty Spence*. Belfast. Blackstaff Press.

Hamill, Heather, 2010 *The hoods: crime and punishment in Belfast*. Princeton. Princeton University Press.

Jenkins, Richard, 1983 *Lads, citizens and ordinary kids: working-class youth life-styles in Belfast*. London. Routledge and Kegan Paul.

McDonald, Henry, 2019 *Two souls*. Kildare. Merrion.

McDonald, Henry, 2004 *Colours: Ireland – from bombs to boom.* Edinburgh. Mainstream.

McKee, Brian, 2020 *Ardoyne '69: stories of struggle and hope.* Dublin. Red Stripe.

Mott, Toby, 2017 *Punk troubles: Northern Ireland.* New York. Dashwood Books.

Mulvenna, Gareth, 2016 *Tartan gangs and paramilitaries: the loyalist backlash.* Liverpool. Liverpool University Press.

O'Connell, Sean, 2006 'From Toad of Toad Hall to the "death drivers" of Belfast: an exploratory history of "joyriding"', *British Journal of Criminology*, vol. 46, no. 3, 455–69.

NOTES

[1] Roy Garland, *Gusty Spence* (Belfast, 2001), 28.

[2] Bill Osgerby, 'Here come the Teds', *Museum of Youth Culture*, https://museumofyouthculture.com/teds/ (accessed 2 Aug. 2021).

[3] *Belfast News Letter*, 8 and 10 June 1955.

[4] Stuart Bailie, *Trouble songs: music and conflict in Northern Ireland* (Belfast, 2018), 14–15.

[5] Robert Niblock, '1955–1972' (n.d., copy provided to author from personal archive).

[6] Ibid.

[7] Brian McKee, *Ardoyne '69: stories of struggle and hope* (Dublin, 2020), 114–15.

[8] Gareth Mulvenna, *Tartan gangs and paramilitaries: the loyalist backlash* (Liverpool, 2016).

[9] Cited in John Darby and Geoffrey Morris, *Intimidation in housing* (Belfast, 1974), 12.

[10] Desmond Bell, *Acts of union: youth culture and sectarianism in Northern Ireland* (Basingstoke, 1990), 23.

[11] Sex Pistols, 'Anarchy in the UK', *Never mind the bollocks, here's the Sex Pistols* (Virgin Records, 1977).

[12] Toby Mott, *Punk troubles: Northern Ireland* (New York, 2017), 94.

[13] Henry McDonald, *Colours: Ireland from – bombs to boom* (Edinburgh, 2004).

[14] Ibid., 65.

[15] Daniel Dylan Wray, 'Sugar Sweet: the pilled-up rave that united Belfast during the Troubles' *The Guardian*, 1 Jan. 2020, https://www.theguardian.com/music/2020/jan/01/sugar-sweet-rave-united-belfast-david-holmes-iain-mccready (accessed 2 Aug. 2021).

SHOPS
Visit our Upstairs Dept for BOOKS PAPERBACKS
Pure gold...
GARDNERS AGAINST GAYS!
-BUY YOUR GIRLIE MAGS,
FREEZING

Out of the shadows
One hundred years of LGBT life in Northern Ireland

TOM HULME

On 11 February 2020, Robyn Peoples and Sharni Edwards tied the knot in Northern Ireland's debut same-sex wedding. Five years after law reform in the Republic of Ireland and six years behind the rest of the UK, same-sex couples were finally able to have their love acknowledged in the eyes of the law. Back in 2015, the Northern Ireland Assembly had considered the issue for the fifth time and a majority had belatedly voted for legalisation, only to be blocked by the DUP invoking the petition of concern. Just over two years later the assembly collapsed, so it took the intervention of MPs at Westminster to legislate for equal marriage. It was politicians elsewhere who gained those rights for the LGBT community – a feeling that gay men who came of age in the 1960s and 1970s will sadly remember all too well.

Jeff Dudgeon protesting Gardner's non-stocking of *Gay News* (1977).

When Northern Ireland was created in 1921, its governing bodies continued to enforce the long-standing British laws that regulated the 'crimes' of homosexuality. Consensual sex between men was punished under the Criminal Law Amendment Act of 1885, which gave up to two years' imprisonment with hard labour. Oscar Wilde was the most famous victim of this act, but it was the Belfast Conservative Unionist MP Edward de Cobain who became its first high-profile scalp in 1893. Sex between women had almost been criminalised in 1921, but MPs had dropped the idea, afraid that drawing attention to lesbianism would only inspire curiosity. By no means was women's desire for each other encouraged, but it flew under the radar of the law and so is mostly unrecorded in Northern Ireland before the gay liberation movement of the 1970s.

Belfast has been home to a male cruising culture since at least the 1880s. Busy streets, dark alleyways, public toilets and sprawling parks all provided opportunities for men seeking other men, from the dockworker to the diplomat (as Roger Casement's salacious diaries confirm).[1] Asking the right question or looking a certain way could lead to a sexual liaison, often in public but sometimes behind closed doors. We only know these encounters happened because of the rare occasion a member of the public reported a man to the authorities, or a policeman walking his beat stumbled across two men *in flagrante*. The heavily stretched RIC (later RUC) had more pressing matters than hunting homosexuals, so arrests before the 1950s usually came by chance rather than through any great feat of detective work. Take the case of James O'Neill in 1928: he made the mistake of fondling Hugh Stitt in a public crowd and promising him 'I can relieve you ... I've been with men before.' Stitt was not interested and led O'Neill straight into the arms of the police.[2]

Men could be brash, despite the risk of arrest, but there was also the danger of assault or blackmail. Terence Moore, a middle-aged man living in Coalisland, fell victim to the provocative advances of a younger man, who then demanded money for several months. Moore could not take this 'torture' and committed suicide by throwing himself in the town's canal in 1933, but not before he had penned a detailed letter to the police, signing off: 'God forgive him and me for my downfall.' The press and jury were shocked by the blackmailer's behaviour and he was given three years in prison – a longer sentence than Moore would have received for his own 'crime'.[3]

Other ways of meeting men depended on the written word. William 'Ernie' Smyth was a young Belfast clerk and a self-styled Wildean aesthete who recorded his discerning taste in music, art and men in widely sent letters. He used a London-based personal-advert magazine called *The Link* to find pen pals; it was shut down in the fallout from his arrest in the early 1920s.[4] The *Belfast Telegraph*'s classified pages, perhaps in the editors' ignorance, were a more local venue for men seeking men. Coded entries of 'lonely bachelors' looking for 'a chum' were common from the 1920s to 1960s, before more specialist publications – like the UK-wide *Gay News* or the Northern Ireland-based *Gay Star* – began catering for the community in the 1970s and 1980s (though some local libraries and newsagents, like Gardner's, refused to stock them, leading to activist protests at their doors).

Before the Second World War life was a secretive and complicated affair for LGBT people in Northern Ireland. Only a couple of men a year were unfortunate enough to stand trial for homosexual offences, but an out-and-proud identity was not on the agenda, especially for lesbians and transgender people. That began to change in the late 1950s, both for the good and for the bad. In 1958, the year after the Wolfenden Committee was appointed by the British government to investigate the 'public menace' of homosexuality, 17 men in Lurgan had found themselves dragged before the courts in a sting operation.[5] Anxieties throughout the UK in the shadow of the Cold War had led to an alarming growth in arrests, and the sense that homosexuality, now front-page news and an open topic of conversation, could no longer be ignored. The ensuing discussion about law reform had contrary effects: it brought same-sex desire into public view and started a journey towards legal equality, but created new distinctions between acceptable and unacceptable sexual behaviour.

Northern Ireland got the worst of both worlds in the 1960s: no extension of the act in 1967 that finally legalised sex between men in England and Wales, but all the public outrage about morality and decency that the reform debates had fuelled. Overzealous policing – even if often it was one rabid constable after an easy target rather than any official crackdown – meant living a gay life in Northern Ireland had become much riskier. But amidst intolerance a subculture was emerging. In 1962, *Le guide gris*, a gay travel newsletter published in New York, had a brief entry for Belfast: 'Royal Avenue Bar – corner of Royal Avenue and Rosemary Street – moderately dressed – all classes'.[6] Attached to the hotel of the same name, this bar was brightly lit with plastic yellow seats, staffed by two former armed-services men who 'stood for no nonsense' and frequented by a brave band of 19 men and a lesbian couple.[7]

One secretive bar did not equal an immediate clamour for social and political change, however. Antony Grey, a homosexual law-reform champion in Britain, was invited to Belfast in 1969 by the Samaritans and the Northern Ireland Association for Mental Health, who hoped to learn how best to support gay people. The Elmwood Association was then set up but, being dominated by heterosexual legal and medical professionals rather than LGBT people, it was a lame duck and already ceased activity in 1971.[8] Yet the times were changing and an emboldened activist base – spurred on by the global radical shift in student politics, the gay-liberation movement in Britain and North America, liberal Christianity and the civil-rights movement at home – began to organise.[9] The Gay Liberation Society, run out of Queen's University, Belfast Students' Union (though not limited to students), came first in 1972; the Union for Sexual Freedoms in Ireland followed in 1974 (collapsing in 1975 following internal feuds); Cara-Friend – a much-needed telephone switchboard, letter and befriending service – started in 1974 (and was funded by the Department of Health and Social Security (DHSS) from 1975 onwards); and the Northern Ireland Gay Rights Association (NIGRA) followed in 1975 (its inaugural meeting memorialised in John Hewitt's poem 'As you like it'). Many organisations were dominated by men, but lesbian women were making their voices heard too, especially through the women's-liberation movement. A Belfast chapter of Sappho was formed in the 1970s, Northern Irish women were involved in *Women's News* in the 1980s and the zine *Muff Monsters on Prozac* brought a more radical queer edge in the 1990s.

Founder members of the AIDS Helpline (1985/6), from LEFT-TO-RIGHT: Julie MacRea, Colin Magee, Suzanne Johnston, Brian Gilmore, Stella Mahon, Mary Torney, Mike Young, Doug Sobey.

The border question and any alignment of gay rights with other movements, such as Gays Against Imperialism, occasionally led to tensions. But all-Ireland cooperation also took place (such as at the pivotal conference on sexuality at the New University of Ulster's Coleraine campus in 1973) and sectarianism on the scene was certainly rarer than in broader society. After the ring of steel had been erected in Belfast during the Troubles, it was often only gays who went into the city centre after dark, leading to sometimes amusing – but often terrifying – anecdotes about encounters with the British army. In the mid-1970s, the Royal Avenue Hotel's elegant ballroom started hosting gay discos run by a couple, Jim Kempson and Ernie Thompson, who had fallen foul of another sting operation in Bangor in 1967 (they later ran the Chariot Rooms, the first gay-owned venue). The Students' Union at Queen's University also ran popular discos.[10] Other venues started to crop up in Belfast too, from the Casanova Club and the Europa's Whip and Saddle bar in the 1970s to the Crow's Nest and the Carpenter Club in the 1980s. Most bars burned brightly only for a short time, victims to both bombings and the economic realities of a society at war.

A change in the law was slower to arrive than a more open gay culture. The RUC had first backed off after the law changed in England and Wales, quietly ignoring what men did together in their own homes. But in 1976, as the gay-rights movement began to gather steam, they resumed intimidation tactics (after receiving a public complaint from a mother who read her gay son's love letters) by arresting around 20 activists; eventually, the attorney general in London stepped in to ensure the politically embarrassing case did not reach court. Campaigns for legalisation made few inroads into Northern Ireland's mainstream political culture and Ian Paisley's 'Save Ulster from Sodomy' campaign (1977–83) bolstered popular homophobia (despite the valiant efforts of counter-protestors, who wore 'Save Sodomy from Ulster' T-shirts at the National Union of Students' annual Lesbian and Gay Conference in Belfast in 1983). Jeff Dudgeon, supported by NIGRA, eventually took the UK government to the European Court of Human Rights and, in 1982, sex in private between men aged 21 and over was finally legalised in Northern Ireland after a ruling by a body beyond its borders (it took further campaigns in the 1990s to equalise the age of consent).

Legalisation was not the end of discrimination for the gay community in Northern Ireland.[11] Several homophobic murders during the Troubles remain unsolved, like the 1997 killing of David Templeton (a Presbyterian minister outed by *Sunday Life*). None of the major political parties showed themselves

Foyle Pride in
Derry/Londonderry
(2019).

to be particularly tolerant in these difficult decades, but there was an undeniably virulent strain of homophobia in the DUP. Religious conservatism and especially the teachings of the Free Presbyterian Church have meant that opinions on same-sex relationships were slow to change – despite the efforts of the Northern Ireland Council on Religion and Sexuality (later Gay Christian Fellowship and, by 2007, Changing Attitude Ireland).[12] More recent comments from DUP politicians about so-called gay-conversion therapy demonstrate that old beliefs can die hard, so it is not surprising that many LGBT people continue to emigrate for the freedom of more liberal societies.

Over the last couple of decades many organisations, events and venues have risen up to demand progress or provide services for the LGBT community: the Rainbow Project (1994), which extended community services to Derry through the Foyle LGBT Centre (2003); the Lesbian Advocacy Services Initiative (1999, rebranded HEReNI in 2012); the Outburst Queer Arts Festival (2007–present); and the Kremlin (1999), Northern Ireland's longest-running LGBT venue. Support for transgender people has also grown. There had been a venue for 'transvestites' in Ballygowan as early as 1970 and monthly meetings hosted by Cara-Friend from the mid-1970s. In 1991, the Belfast Butterfly Club was founded as a self-help group and still provides a safe space for transgender people today. The trans youth service GenderJam NI appeared in 2013, the Belfast Trans Resource Centre in 2016, and TransgenderNI in 2018. Nonetheless, discrimination remains a serious problem.

Just four years ago, uniformed members of the Police Service of Northern Ireland (PSNI) marched in Belfast Pride for the first time. Given the historical role of the police in persecuting LGBT people, they were not welcomed by all. But their inclusion, along with several Christian churches, shows how far attitudes have changed. The Pride parade in 2019 brought out 50,000 cheering spectators – an unimaginable number for the organisers of the inaugural Pride in 1991, when a defiant band of 100 activists took to the streets in front of a much more hostile audience. Other places also hold Pride festivals: Derry/Londonderry (since 2010), Newry (since 2012) and Mid-Ulster (2021). Progress has often been slow and uneven, but LGBT people in Northern Ireland will no longer accept a life in the shadows.

FURTHER READING

Duggan, Marian, 2012 *Queering conflict: examining lesbian and gay experiences of homophobia in Northern Ireland*. Farnham. Ashgate.
Ferriter, Diarmaid, 2009 *Occasions of sin: sex and society in modern Ireland*. London. Profile.
Hulme, Tom, 2021 'Queer Belfast during the First World War: masculinity and same-sex desire in the Irish city', *Irish Historical Studies*, vol. 45, no. 168.
Lewis, Brian, 2005 'The queer life and afterlife of Roger Casement', *Journal of the History of Sexuality*, vol. 14, no. 4, 363–82.
McDonagh, Patrick, 2019 '"Homosexuality is not a problem – it doesn't do you any harm and can be lots of fun": students and gay rights activism in Irish universities, 1970s–1980s', *Irish Economic and Social History*, vol. 46, 111–41.
Murgu, Cal, 2017 '"Innocence is as innocence does": Anglo Irish politics, masculinity and the de Cobain gross indecency scandal, 1891–3', *Gender and History*, vol. 29, no. 2, 309–28.

NOTES

[1] Jeffrey Dudgeon, *Roger Casement: the Black Diaries: with a study of his background, sexuality, and Irish political life* (Belfast, 2002).
[2] Belfast Crown and Peace, records of Belfast Crown Court (PRONI, 1/1/2/86/64).
[3] *Belfast Telegraph*, 26 July 1933.
[4] Metropolitan Police records (TNA, 3/283).
[5] *Belfast Telegraph*, 18 Dec. 1958.

6   *Le guide gris* (3rd ed., New York, 1962).

7   Malachi O'Doherty, *Fifty years on: the Troubles and the struggle for change in Northern Ireland* (London, 2019), 185–6.

8   'Conference on social needs, York University', 1970 (Hall-Carpenter Archives, London, Albany Trust papers).

9   Papers of Cara-Friend (PRONI, D4437) and NIGRA (PRONI, D3672); Moya Morris (ed.), *Threads: stories of lesbian life in Northern Ireland in the 1970s and 1980s* (Belfast, 2013).

10 *Belfast Telegraph*, 1 Aug. 1967.

11 Marian Duggan, *Queering conflict: examining lesbian and gay experiences of homophobia in Northern Ireland* (Farnham, 2012).

12 Richard O'Leary, 'The faithful underground: gay Christian activism in Ireland in the 1970s and 1980s', talk delivered at Institute of Irish Studies, Queen's University Belfast, 21 Oct. 2019.

'Over' by Sophia Campbell, courtesy of the artist.

This painting appeared in 'Emerging Artists' in the exhibition *Portrait of Northern Ireland: neither an elegy nor a manifesto* (2021)

Controlling women's bodies
in Northen Ireland

1921–2021

LEANNE McCORMICK

In April 2021, following a 431 to 89 vote in the House of
Commons, the House of Lords at Westminster passed
regulations to direct the commissioning of abortion
services in Northern Ireland. Changes to the abortion
laws in Northern Ireland came into force in March 2020;
however, at the time of writing the full commissioning of
services has yet to take place, with a DUP MP stating that
Northern Ireland has developed 'over more than 50 years,
our own approach to valuing the unborn, choosing life
and having distinctive life-affirming laws'.[1] Catholic and
Protestant church authorities are united in their

(ORIGINAL CAPTION): Abortion-rights demonstrators march through
the streets of Belfast ahead of a meeting of the Stormont Assembly
on abortion rights and gay marriage (21 Oct. 2019).

(CHARLES MCQUILLAN/STRINGER) GETTY IMAGES

condemnation of the legal changes, revealing a unity around issues concerning female reproductive choice and pregnancy that has existed from the establishment of Northern Ireland in 1921.[2] As the debate surrounding abortion laws demonstrates, Northern Irish political and religious authorities have regularly positioned the state as morally superior to other parts of the United Kingdom and with a population that did not want changes to legislation on issues such as abortion, divorce or homosexuality.

Across the century, female sexuality in Northern Ireland has been regulated in a variety of formal and informal ways. The techniques employed and the attitudes towards female sexuality were not only driven by gender and class, but also influenced by the wider political, social and religious situation in Northern Ireland. All sections of the community in Northern Ireland based much of their identity upon the maintenance of high moral standards, particularly with regards to female behaviour. Women were seen as representing the communities, so their perceived moral purity and good behaviour was essential to promoting the image that was required. This chapter will focus on a number of areas relating to reproduction and the female body, demonstrating the unity of attitudes that have persisted across the century.

In the new Northern Ireland, there was across society a condemnation of women whose behaviour failed to meet the required social expectations. Religious authorities, both Protestant and Catholic, were keen to establish that the most important roles for women were as wives and mothers, particularly in the upheaval following the First World War and partition, and to express their concerns about the behaviour of young women and declining morals.[3]

Across class and religious divides one of the main causes of anxiety was pregnancy outside marriage. For most of the century for which Northern Ireland has existed, there was stigma and shame attached to unmarried mothers. Lorna Goldstrom, who established the Ulster Pregnancy Information Service (later becoming the Ulster Pregnancy Advisory Association (UPAA)) in 1971, which provided abortion advice, writing in the *The Guardian* in March 1972, explained that a key feature of Northern Irish society was that the 'fear of forfeiting "respectability" goes deep, frighteningly deep'.[4]

Marianvale, Newry.

The importance of maintaining respectability at all costs is clearly seen in the establishment and operation of mother-and-baby homes in Northern Ireland, with the last home closing in 1992.[5] A number of these institutions were established before partition, including the Belfast Midnight Mission/Rescue and Maternity Home, Malone Place and the Church of Ireland Rescue League Rescue Home. By the first decades of the twentieth century the Salvation Army were beginning to focus their attention on the unmarried mother and a dedicated home for unmarried mothers was opened at Thorndale, off the Antrim Road in Belfast, in 1921. The other main Protestant home, Hopedene, opened in 1943. Provision for unmarried mothers, like so much voluntary provision, was on religiously segregated lines. The first home dedicated for Catholic unmarried mothers, Mater Dei, operated by the Legion of Mary, opened in 1942, followed by two homes run by the Good Shepherd Sisters, Marianville in Belfast in 1950 and Marianvale in Newry in 1955. It is estimated that over 10,500 women entered mother-and-baby homes in Northern Ireland between 1921 and 1992, but this does not include unmarried mothers who entered the workhouses before their closure in 1948, so the true number is considerably higher.

There were a variety of reasons why women entered the homes. Often familial pressure was an important factor, reflecting the upset, disappointment and loss of respectability an illegitimate pregnancy was often seen to bring. Protestant and Catholic clergy were closely involved in the operation of the homes and in the direct and indirect placement of women and girls in them. There was clear condemnation from religious authorities regarding unmarried mothers and certainty about the need for mother-and-baby homes to place these women and girls in. The *Mother and Baby Homes and Magdalene Laundries in Northern Ireland, 1922–1990: report* (January 2021) has demonstrated how these institutions were generally cold and unsympathetic to the women who entered, that many women were made to engage in manual work well into their final trimester and left unprepared for the experience of giving birth. A quarter of babies left mother-and-baby homes with their mothers, but the majority were either placed in institutions, adopted or fostered, reflecting both the lack of support for single mothers keeping their children and the prevailing ideology that this was best for children. Mother-and-baby homes were not unique to the island of Ireland but, north and south of the border, they lasted longer and admitted higher numbers than other countries.[6]

While there was condemnation of the unmarried mother, there was limited support or encouragement for family planning or abortion services within Northern Ireland. Writing about their work providing abortion advice in the 1970s, the UPAA blamed a lack of sex education for unwanted pregnancies. They argued:

> If those who condemn abortion so loudly and with such a considerable amount of energy would but their resources towards campaigning of better sex education programmes and much more publicity regarding contraception, then perhaps the need for abortion which they so vigorous oppose might be decreased considerably.[7]

That this situation had not dramatically improved 40 years later is evidenced by the damming report in 2018 from the Convention on Elimination of All Forms of Discrimination Against Women (CEDAW). The report stated:

> the inadequacy of state-provided family planning support, as driven by socioreligious considerations, coupled with a political culture that circumscribes the role of women, subjects women and girls in Northern Ireland to double jeopardy, effectively depriving them of any control over their fertility.[8]

In terms of introducing family-planning services, Northern Ireland consistently lagged behind the rest of the UK and, while contraception was never banned (as it was south of the border), it was not actively encouraged. A Marie Stopes clinic opened in Belfast in 1936 but closed little over a decade later. It faced religious opposition from the Catholic Church and was never able to generate support across the political or religious spectrum.[9] Following its closure, Dr Olive Anderson contacted the Family Planning Association (FPA) in London in 1950 to discuss opening a clinic in Belfast. After a year of negotiating, she was able to open a clinic in Malone Place in 1951, which was considered to be a Protestant hospital in an attempt to avoid antagonising Catholic opinion. Those involved in running the Belfast Women's Welfare Clinic, as it was known, were so concerned about keeping a low profile and not drawing attention to their activities that they avoided becoming official members of the FPA in order not to embarrass the Hospitals Authority, which had given them premises.[10]

The Northern Ireland Family Planning Association (NIFPA) was established in 1964 and, likewise, were reluctant to publicise their services for fear of attracting religious opposition. In any discussion of their activities they were keen to emphasise that they gave advice to Catholic patients about the rhythm method and were sensitive to patients' beliefs. Dr Joyce Neill, chairperson of NIFPA, emphasised the feelings on family planning in Northern Ireland in a letter to the FPA in London in 1966, arguing that not only was the government trying to 'appease our "oppressed" Roman Catholic minority, but we have a strong Calvinistic element to deal with, to whom we appear as the Scarlet Woman in person'.[11] In the Northern Ireland parliament, in discussions about a grant made to the NIFPA in June 1968, Harry Diamond MP (Republican Labour Party) was angry that there had been no discussion of the issue in the house and pointed out that there was 'substantial division in the community on these matters'. He contended that the term 'family planning' 'is a euphemism for artificial birth control and the promotion of abortions. In my judgement there is no right to use public funds in this connection.'[12]

There was a long-held suspicion that family-planning clinics were promoting or carrying out abortions. The Marie Stopes clinic in Belfast in the 1930s and 1940s recorded women coming to the clinic thinking that it offered abortions.[13] This, along with the court cases relating to abortions in Northern Ireland and the number of women who travelled to Great Britain after 1967 to access abortion following its legalisation there, indicated that even though politicians and church leaders claimed that people in Northern Ireland did not want abortions, the actions of women revealed a very different situation.

The cases that come before the courts relating to abortion generally arise when something has gone wrong and obviously only represent a small proportion of women who successfully terminate or attempt to abort pregnancies. In Belfast, the 31 cases that came before the courts between 1921 and 1968 reveal the wider networks of knowledge that existed relating to abortion and how regularly women used a variety of methods to ensure that they were not pregnant. These often followed a pattern of escalation – from steps to try and regulate menstruation to the point following 'quickening' (when the baby was first felt to move) at around 16 weeks' gestation.[14] Drinking gin, jumping off steps, taking hot baths and drinking castor oil, amongst others, were all referred to as attempts to bring on periods. If these did not work, the next step was often drugs of various kinds, including patent medicines such as Dr Raispail's Female Pills and Beecham's Pills. These were widely advertised in newspapers as being able to remove 'obstructions' and regulate the female system. They were taken ostensibly to regulate menstruation but were effectively and legally abortifacients. Also referenced in the records was the use of a syringe with hot soapy water or a disinfectant. Douching was commonly used for female hygiene purposes, and by medical professionals as well, to abort a pregnancy. It could, however, have tragic consequences if misused. Five women died from the use of a syringe when attempting to procure an abortion.[15]

If none of the previous methods was successful, visiting an abortionist for an operation using some sort of instrument was often the final step. In a number of cases, medical professionals, doctors, nurses and midwives were involved. Undoubtedly, for those who could afford to pay their fees, there have always been doctors who were willing to carry out abortions. Max Goldstrom, one of the founders of the UPAA, wrote of how in the 1960s in Northern Ireland there were several backstreet abortionists at work, but hardly any prosecutions. One medically trained man was apparently recommended by the police to women who had become pregnant through rape. He also stated that in 1981 a doctor who was carrying out backstreet abortions was prosecuted after one of his patients died, and his sentence 'was astonishingly light', suggesting there was some tolerance for his activities.[16]

Abortions such as these, however, were clearly against the law. The Abortion Act of 1967, passed in England, Scotland and Wales, was not extended to Northern Ireland; attempts to extend the legislation were always rejected due to the 'long standing consensus of the dominant political parties against abortion'.[17] The law in Northern Ireland continued to be based on the 1861 Offences Against the Person Act, which criminalised any woman who had an abortion as well as anyone who tried to help her. It was further defined in 1938, following the trial of Aleck Bourne, which provided a legal defence for doctors who performed abortions if they believed it was for the good of a woman's physical or mental health. This was interpreted very narrowly in Northern Ireland and became increasingly restrictive over time, with only several hundred legal abortions being performed in the 1970s and 1980s and only 12 in 2017/18.[18]

Because of these legal restrictions, Northern Irish women had to travel to Great Britain for an abortion, with estimates given of over 60,000 women since 1967. It was not until 2017 that women from Northern Ireland were able to access abortions free through the NHS. Prior to this they had to pay the costs themselves.[19] The UPAA, which was set up in 1971, advised women about travelling to England for an abortion, offered counselling and made appointments for women who wanted to proceed with the operation. Various campaigning groups were also established in the 1970s and 1980s to fight for changes in the law; in 1996 Alliance for Choice was formed, which has remained prominent in the campaign for legal change.

Various anti-abortion groups were also established, a number of whom were extreme in their activities, picketing outside the premises of the UPAA and other family-planning providers and in town centres. In July 1999 the UPAA premises were broken into and a fire was started. While the pro-life group Precious Life denied any involvement, they welcomed the subsequent closure of the UPAA as a 'great victory'.[20] In 2021 pro-life groups are still picketing family-planning and sexual-health centres.

There were attempts to introduce guidelines relating to the termination of pregnancies for the Northern Ireland Executive in 2016 by the then-health minister, David Ford. However, the collapse of the executive in 2017 prevented these being implemented. Following the condemnatory 2018 CEDAW report, as well as legal challenges, attention was refocused on Westminster to legislate. Campaigning was also strengthened by the May 2018 vote in the Republic of Ireland to repeal the eighth amendment and allow abortion on request within the first 12 weeks of pregnancy. This also led to Sinn Féin reversing its policy on abortion. In July 2019 a proposal from

Labour MP Stella Creasy to decriminalise abortion in Northern Ireland if devolution was not restored by 21 October 2019 was supported by 332 votes to 99 in the House of Commons. Devolution was not restored until January 2020 and in March of that year the details of the new legal framework for abortion regulations were published. There continued to be delays in commissioning abortion services and, in March 2021, a majority of members of the legislative assembly at Stormont voted to amend the law to prevent abortions in the cases of non-fatal disabilities.

The situation changed again when, in April 2021, the House of Commons and House of Lords at Westminster approved regulations which will allow the Northern Ireland secretary of state to compel the Northern Ireland Department of Health to commission abortion services. It remains to be seen what changes this will actually bring for Northern Irish women in a century that has brought more continuity than change so far. The population's view of itself as morally distinct from secular Great Britain has persisted, as have attempts to control women's bodies.

FURTHER READING

Delay, Cara, 2018 'Kitchens and kettles: domestic spaces, ordinary things, and female networks in Irish abortion history, 1922–1949', *Journal of Women's History*, vol. 30, no. 4, 11–34.

Earner-Byrne, Lindsey and Urquhart, Diane, 2019 *The Irish abortion journey, 1920–2018*. Cham. Palgrave.

Hill, Myrtle, 2003 *Women in Ireland: a century of change*. Belfast. Blackstaff Press.

McCormick, Leanne, 2009 *Regulating sexuality: women in twentieth-century Northern Ireland*. Manchester. Manchester University Press.

NOTES

[1] House of Commons, Abortion (Northern Ireland) Regulations 2021, *Hansard: Commons*, vol. 639 (26 Apr. 2021), col. 18.

[2] Lisa Smyth, 'The cultural politics of sexuality and reproduction in Northern Ireland', *Sociology*, vol. 40, no. 4 (2006), 668.

[3] Leanne McCormick, *Regulating sexuality: women in twentieth-century Northern Ireland* (Manchester, 2009), 98–101.

[4] *The Guardian*, 1 Mar. 1972.

[5] For more on mother and baby homes in Northern Ireland, see Leanne McCormick and Sean O'Connell with Olivia Dee and John Privilege, *Mother and Baby Homes and Magdalene Laundries in Northern Ireland, 1922–1990: report, January 2021* (Belfast, 2021), https://www.health-ni.gov.uk/publication-research-report-mbhml (accessed 2 Aug. 2021).

6   McCormick and O'Connell, *Mother and Baby Homes*. For more on mother and
    baby homes in the Republic of Ireland see *Mother and Baby Homes
    Commission of Investigation final report: 30 October 2020* (Dublin, 2020),
    https://www.gov.ie/en/publication/d4b3d-final-report-of-ther-commission-of-
    investigation-into-mother-and-baby-homes/?referrer=http://www.gov.ie/report/
    (accessed 2 Aug. 2021).
7   UPAA, *Abortion, the first six years in N. Ireland, 1971–1976* (Belfast, 1976), 4.
8   UN CEDAW, *Report of the inquiry concerning the United Kingdom of Great
    Britain and Northern Ireland under article 8 of the Optional Protocol to the
    Convention on the Elimination of All Forms of Discrimination against Women,
    CEDAW* (New York, 2018), 12.
9   Greta Jones, 'Marie Stopes in Ireland: the Mother's Clinic in Belfast, 1936–47',
    Social History of Medicine, vol. 5, no. 2 (1992), 276.
10 Leanne McCormick, '"The Scarlet Woman in person": the establishment of a
    family planning service in Northern Ireland, 1950–1974', *Social History of
    Medicine*, vol. 21, no. 2 (2008), 350.
11 Dr Joyce Neill to London FPA, 4 Feb. 1966 (PRONI, NIFPA correspondence,
    D/3543/3/1).
12 *Hansard NI (Commons)*, vol. 69 (session 1967–8), col. 2047 (6 June 1968).
13 Jones, 'Marie Stopes in Ireland', 259–60.
14 Leanne McCormick '"No sense of wrongdoing": abortion in Belfast
    1917–1967', *Journal of Social History*, vol. 49, no. 1 (2015), 129.
15 Ibid., 130.
16 J.M. Goldstrom, 'Abortion and the law in N. Ireland', *Scope*, July/Aug. 1981, 8.
17 Fiona Bloomer and Eileen Fegan, 'Critiquing recent abortion law and policy in
    Northern Ireland', *Critical Social Policy*, vol. 34, no. 1 (2014), 110–11.
18 Sally Sheldon, Jane O'Neill, Clare Parker and Gayle Davis, '"Too much, too
    indigestible, too fast"? The decades of struggle for abortion law reform in
    Northern Ireland', *The Modern Law Review*, vol. 83, no. 4 (2020), 763.
19 Ibid., 765.
20 *Irish Times*, 5 Aug. 1999.

Afterword

IAN McBRIDE

How can we find constructive ways of commemorating the creation of Northern Ireland one hundred years ago? There is no easy answer to this question. The partition of Ireland was a flawed attempt to reconcile the aspirations of unionists and nationalists. The responsibility for its deficiencies lies with decision-makers in Belfast, in London and, to some extent, in Dublin also. In many respects the constitutional settlement of 1920–2 was the antithesis of the peace process of the 1990s. It was the outcome of violence and the threat of violence. When the Northern Ireland parliament was inaugurated in June 1921, the backdrop was grim: guerrilla warfare and state reprisals in the south, vicious intercommunal rioting and sectarian assassinations in the north. Neither unionists nor nationalists were prepared to recognise the legitimacy of each other's political allegiances. Each regarded the historical and cultural traditions of the other as invalid. The legacy of violent confrontation and political polarisation poisoned the new political structures established in 1921.

'I Hear Dogs Barking', 2005, by Emma Connolly.

Courtesy of the Arts Council of Northern Ireland and the artist. This painting appeared in 'A New Tradition' in the exhibition *Portrait of Northern Ireland: neither an elegy nor a manifesto* (2021)

Pҡesident Michael D. Higgins recently urged that the organising principle in Irish commemorations should be 'a hospitality of narratives' – a phrase borrowed from the philosopher Richard Kearney, which signals an openness to different stories and different perspectives on our historical experience.[1] But hospitality comes more easily to societies that feel at home with themselves; it requires hard work in the north, where neither community feels that its right to belong can be taken for granted. In the south – for the most part – the decade of centenaries has been a remarkably positive and productive process. The period between the queen's visit and the UK's referendum on EU membership provided an unusually auspicious moment for the Irish government to acknowledge the diversity of Irish allegiances during the First World War, whilst simultaneously affirming the value of its own revolutionary origins in the Easter Rising of 1916. The guiding precepts of the centenary commemoration were laudable: historical accuracy, mutual respect, inclusiveness and reconciliation. This spirit was displayed, to take just one example, in the Remembrance Wall at Glasnevin Cemetery – where the names of all those who died were recorded, irrespective of their background or their political allegiance.

But this latitude reflects decades of consensus about the fundamental structures of the state. The political scientist John Coakley observed 20 years ago that nationalism in the south was no longer Catholic or communal in character; that a new form of state patriotism had emerged, comfortable with the political and territorial framework of a 26-county Ireland.[2] In the years before 2016, Irish political issues, most notably the referendum on marriage equality, were only tangentially related to the Irish revolution of 1916–22. Consequently, the aim of the centenary – in the words of the Expert Advisory Group – was 'to broaden sympathies, without having to abandon loyalties'. At the same time, the group acknowledged that 'the state cannot be expected to be neutral about the events that led to its formation'.[3] This kind of balancing act is not possible north of the border.

There is, moreover, a deeper obstacle: Northern Ireland was not designed as a joint endeavour. Partition was imposed on one community in Northern Ireland to satisfy the demands of the other. The contours of the border reflect the balance of power in 1921 rather than the niceties of demography. So the centenary unavoidably serves as a reminder to northern nationalists of the decades of disempowerment that followed. A hundred years later, the task of reconceiving Northern Ireland as a shared political space still challenges political imaginations as well as political wills.

The boundary question

On 8 December 1925 Winston Churchill told the British House of Commons: 'The Irish question will only be finally settled when the human question is finally settled.'[4] On that day the tripartite agreement between the three governments of the United Kingdom, the Irish Free State and Northern Ireland was announced, revoking the powers of the Boundary Commission and confirming the existing border of Northern Ireland. Churchill's cryptic aphorism comes to mind because it encapsulates an important truth: the partition of Ireland was not an anachronism or an anomaly in the Europe that emerged from the cataclysms of the First World War, but part of a very modern political dilemma. The intractability of the Irish question was just one example of the problems created by the rise of nationalism as a global force – by the dangerous fantasy that each sovereign state must be the political embodiment of a homogeneous national population.[5]

One useful function of historians is to remind us that our predicaments are rarely as particular as we think. The unprecedented strains created by the Great War not only split apart the union of Britain and Ireland; they also brought about the collapse of the great continental empires ruled over for centuries by the Habsburgs, the Romanovs and the Ottomans. In the years between 1919 and 1923 the European political landscape was fundamentally reorganised. The new states of Poland and Czechoslovakia were established, Romania was enlarged, the Saar Basin in Germany and the Baltic port of Danzig were internationalised, and the area around Smyrna (modern Izmir) was awarded to the Greeks. In all these cases, as in Ireland, the wishes of the inhabitants collided with strategic interests and with local political and economic circumstances. The European historian Mark Mazower reminds us that the Paris peace settlement of 1919–23 granted 60 million people a state of their own; but it also turned 25 million people into 'minorities'.[6]

Two contrasts stand out. First, the level and character of violence in the Irish case was relatively low and restrained. Tim Wilson's 2010 book *Frontiers of violence: conflict and identity in Ulster and Upper Silesia, 1918–1922* presents a magisterial comparison of Ulster with Upper Silesia, the industrialised borderland between Germany and Poland, which was also partitioned in the aftermath of the First World War. Between 1918 and 1922 the number of violent deaths was, in proportion to their populations, three times greater in Upper Silesia than in Ulster: an estimated 2,824 fatalities as compared with Ulster's 714.[7] But the character of the violence was equally divergent, with rape, torture and mutilation much more common in Upper Silesia.

An examination of displacement reinforces the point. The number of northern nationalists fleeing south, or to British cities, and of southern unionists leaving Ireland, amounted to tens of thousands. Their stories have been forgotten, although such migration, sometimes forced, altered the demographic make-up of both islands.[8] These movements were dwarfed, however, by the population exchange of one million people between Greece and Turkey. It would be comforting to imagine that the Irish somehow resisted the pressures of communal polarisation more resolutely than their continental counterparts. But the determining feature of the Irish case was that, whereas the German Reich was defeated and the Ottoman and Habsburg empires dismantled, the British empire had emerged from the European war as the only financial and naval power that could rival the United States. Ireland had been sheltered from the total war that swept away political institutions and destroyed economic life on the European mainland. In the aftermath of the Great War, Lloyd George was a key player in shaping the new political boundaries of eastern Europe and the Middle East; no other state was in a position to interfere with his negotiations with Sinn Féin and the Ulster Unionists. The issue of the partition of Ireland was never internationalised.

The other stabilising factor operating in the 1920s was hardly more edifying. On both sides of the border the dominant political factions, fortified by emergency legislation and by a swollen security apparatus, found in the consolidation of power over their respective territories ample compensation for having to downsize their political ambitions. The UVF gunrunner and zealot Fred Crawford produced a leaflet in 1920 entitled *Why I voted for the six counties*, dismissing the protestations of his fellow loyalists and covenanters in Donegal, Cavan and Monaghan. Ireland was a sinking ship, he retorted, and the hard truth was that there was not enough room for all Ulster Protestants on the lifeboat.[9] Southerners could be similarly unsentimental about abandoning their coreligionists to the tyranny of the northern majority. When the Boundary Commission collapsed in 1925 without delivering the expected revision of the border, the republican activist Liam de Róiste noted the indifference of public opinion in his native Cork. The issue of the boundary, he remarked, 'does not enter into our lives in the South'.[10]

Democracy and dynamite

The right to self-determination was the famous maxim to emerge from the post-war settlement. It has subsequently been enshrined in UN declarations as an essential condition for the observance of human rights; it is a fundamental concept in the Good Friday Agreement. To Woodrow Wilson it meant simply government by consent. But, while the US president claimed that self-determination would make the world 'safe for democracy', his secretary of state, Robert Lansing, worried that this new concept was 'loaded with dynamite'.[11] Historians, political scientists and international lawyers have tended to agree, because the doctrine of self-determination raises more questions than it answers. Before the people determine their own future, someone must first determine who the people are. What territorial boundaries are they entitled to claim as their own? What happens where peoples overlap, where one community's claim to self-government becomes entangled with another?

Historians have sometimes presented partition as a case study in how physical force can prevail over democracy. But this view is a deceptive simplification. The actions of unionists, nationalists and republicans were always constrained by their ability to appeal to established principles of legitimacy – not only principles that resonated with their followers at home, but also those accepted by international opinion. The real issue was not between those who accepted democratic values and those who rejected them. The disagreement was about the applicability of democratic government in a divided society.

Sinn Féin claimed that Ireland had a right to nationhood because of its historical continuity, its centuries of resistance to British rule and, above all, its distinctive cultural personality. Arthur Griffith protested in 1920 that self-determination was a matter for nations and peoples, not for mere 'parishes and shires' (that is, the six counties).[12] Éamon de Valera said that giving self-determination to the six counties was to reduce the doctrine to a 'tribalistic' level.[13] The Ulster Protestants were historically, culturally and racially Irish, and they would realise this fact once the lies of British imperialists and Belfast capitalists were exposed. During his American campaign of 1919–20, de Valera explained that 'the people of Ireland constitute a distinct and separate nation, ethnically, historically, and tested by every standard of political science'. None of the new states – Czechoslovakia, Finland, even Poland – could 'even approach the perfection of nationhood manifested by Ireland'.

Ireland had exercised sovereign powers for a thousand years before the invasion of the Danes, he boasted. The Irish nation was 'as homogeneous as any nation upon the earth'. A free Ireland, he asserted without further elaboration, would easily deal with its 'minority problem'.[14]

A survey of just over 300 Protestant clergymen carried out by the *Daily Mail* in 1912 provides a valuable insight into the mindset of that minority. Fifty-four per cent feared for the security of their religion under Home Rule. It is well known that Presbyterians in particular were anxious about the *Ne Temere* decree which declared 'mixed' marriages null and void unless solemnised by a Catholic priest. Reverend David Mitchel of Warrenpoint, incidentally the brother of the republican John Mitchel, believed that Home Rule would inevitably 'lead to the ascendancy of a system always hostile to freedom and toleration'. Forty-two per cent protested that Ulster's industrial economy would be destroyed; 19 per cent warned that Home Rule would disrupt the empire; 15 per cent believed that it would lead to civil war.[15] What

Street party for the Queen's visit (Aug. 1977), Matchett Street/Brussels Street.

is less well known is that these concerns resonated with a large body of opinion in Britain, particularly, but not exclusively, in the northern industrial cities, as an important recent book by Daniel Jackson has established.[16] Sympathy for Ulster Protestants also existed in the West Country, where the nonconformist churches were strong. This, perhaps, explains the otherwise mysterious fact that it was the obscure Cornish MP Thomas Agar-Robartes who first proposed that four counties – Antrim, Down, Londonderry and Armagh – should be excluded from Home Rule in June 1912. The Agar-Robartes amendment was the first time the idea of partition was proposed at Westminster.

The underlying unionist argument was that the Irish did not form a single national unit, but two antagonistic populations separated by religion, ethnic origin and political loyalties. As the Ulster liberal Thomas Sinclair put it: 'There is no national Irish demand for Home Rule, because there never has been and there is no homogeneous Irish nation.'[17] In August 1918 Edward Carson published his own letter to President Wilson, protesting that Ulstermen remained as devoted to the cause of democratic freedom as their eighteenth-century forefathers. Nationalists were welcome to Home Rule, provided that the Ulster Protestants were left alone. In rejecting this compromise, Carson complained, nationalists revealed that their goal was not simply self-government for themselves, but 'coercive domination over us'.[18] Democracy did not offer a peaceful solution to the Ulster conflict so much as equip the belligerents with an new arsenal of ultra-modern weaponry.

A rock of granite

Northern Ireland was founded upon a double standard. In 1912 unionists argued that, under Irish Home Rule, Protestants would be radically disadvantaged. The settlement of 1921 reversed that objection rather than resolving it. Britain awarded to the unionists the maximum area they could effectively control. Little attempt was made to counterbalance unionist majority rule with protections for the minority. But if there could be no justice in an Ireland where Protestants were outnumbered three to one, how could there be justice in a six-county Ulster where Catholics were outnumbered by two to one?

During the treaty negotiations, James Craig reassured his followers that 'Ulster was not a cheese to be nibbled at; it was a rock of granite that would break the teeth of those mice that attempted to bite it'.[19] The illogicality of the six-county border was highlighted in *Ulster and Home Rule: no partition of Ulster*, a pamphlet issued by the Unionist delegates of Cavan, Donegal and Monaghan in April 1920. If the three border counties were to be omitted because of their nationalist majorities, they demanded, then what about Fermanagh and Tyrone? What about Derry City, south Armagh, south Down?[20] Twenty-one local authorities in these nationalist areas swore allegiance to Dáil Éireann. In Derry, where the nationalist council refused to recognise the Belfast parliament, the creation of Craig's rock of granite required that 2,000 British troops be despatched to police a population of 50,000 people. The imposition of the border was therefore experienced as a kind of conquest by many of the communities living along the new international boundary. With the threat of the Boundary Commission hanging over him, and the possibility that its report would recommend the transfer of blocs of territory to the Free State, Craig agreed to the redrawing of local electoral boundaries –

PRONI, D4629/1/6/1

Social Democratic and Labour Party (SDLP) election poster.

gerrymandering – initially as a temporary deviation.[21] Although the Unionist leader won five general elections with large majorities, he failed to articulate a strategy for healing the communal divisions that would eventually overwhelm the parliament he had created.

During the Stormont years Ulster unionists were allowed to treat Northern Ireland as their own exclusive property. It was *their* creation and it existed to protect the values that were specific to them: the survival of the Protestant religion, loyalty to the crown, the British way of life. The assumption was that Northern Ireland – or as they generally preferred to call it, 'Ulster' – had a single unitary personality with its own distinct history. When Craig remarked that Richard Dawson Bates 'knew the mind of Ulster better than almost anyone else', he unthinkingly conformed to the standard rhetorical practice of unionists, which assumed that Catholics and nationalists, at least for political purposes, did not really exist.[22]

• • •

In the decade before 1921, the risk of a civil war in Ireland was taken seriously. The political and social forces working in favour of partition were very powerful. Nobody had a coherent and obviously workable alternative. This collection of essays has illuminated many of the conflicting forces that shaped Northern Ireland. Unionists remained stubbornly blind to the logic of their own argument: if Home Rule was wrong for a divided Ireland, as they repeated insistently, it was surely wrong for a divided 'Ulster' too. Nationalists and republicans continued to dismiss Ulster unionism as a phantom created by British imperialists and Belfast industrialists – it was 'purely a product of British party maneuvering' – to use de Valera's words.[23] There was no glimmer of a 'hospitality of narratives' in the 1920s, nor would there be for many decades to come.

British politicians exhibited their own varieties of myopia and self-delusion. The driving force here was not imperialism, although London naturally sought to protect its geopolitical interests. If anything, the creation of Northern Ireland reflected a kind of psychological decolonisation. Establishing a parliament in Belfast – as opposed to maintaining what we might call 'direct rule' – allowed the government to achieve its overriding aim of removing the Irish question from British politics. The report of Walter Long's committee, which was the basis for the Government of Ireland Act, reasoned that a two-parliament solution would also neutralise the criticism that part of Ireland remained under British control: 'No nationalists would be retained under British rule. All Irishmen would be self-governing.'[24]

Over the decades, the mechanisms of denial and evasion became habitual and the rationalisations more practised. The centenary year has provided an opportunity to interrogate some of these self-serving reflexes. In remembering the apparent certainties of 1921, we must not forget the messy compromises made in the 1990s, and the reasons why it became necessary to abandon inherited belief systems. The challenge for historians, among others, is to ensure that the complex realities of the Irish situation a century ago are not ironed out for political, ideological or therapeutic reasons. Writing as the 'decade of commemorations' began, the late David Fitzpatrick encouraged historians to 'raise awkward issues and, above all, seek to broaden the terms of debate'. As we contemplate the centenary of Northern Ireland, Fitzpatrick's exhortation bears repeating. 'Far from avoiding all forms of judgement,' he advised, historians should try 'to add moral intensity to the ways in which we commemorate and comprehend the past.'[25]

FURTHER READING

Bowman, John, 1989 *De Valera and the Ulster question 1917–1973*. Oxford. Oxford University Press.
Fitzpatrick, David, 1998 *The two Irelands, 1912–1939*. Oxford. Oxford University Press.
Jackson, Alvin, 2003 *Home Rule: an Irish history 1800–2000*. London. Weidenfeld and Nicolson.
MacMillan, Margaret, 2001 *Paris 1919: six months that changed the world*. London. Random House.
O'Leary, Brendan, 2019 *A treatise on Northern Ireland, vol. 2: control*. Oxford. Oxford University Press.
Prott, Volker, 2016 *The politics of self-determination: remaking territories and national identities in Europe, 1917–1923*. Oxford. Oxford University Press.
Townshend, Charles, 2021 *The partition: Ireland divided, 1885–1925*. London. Allen Lane.

NOTES

1 Michael D. Higgins, 'Empire shaped Ireland's past. A century after partition, it still shapes our present', *Guardian*, 11 Feb. 2021.
2 John Coakley, 'Religion, national identity and political change in modern Ireland', *Irish Political Studies*, vol. 17, no. 1 (2002), 4–28.
3 Diarmaid Ferriter, '1916 in 2016: personal reflections of an Irish historian', *Irish Historical Studies*, vol. 42, no. 161 (2018), 161.
4 R.R. James (ed.), *Winston S. Churchill: his complete speeches* (8 vols, London, 1974), iv, 3,791.
5 Eric D. Weitz, 'From the Vienna to the Paris System: international politics and the entangled histories of human rights, forced deportations, and civilizing missions', *The American Historical Review*, vol. 113, no. 5 (2008), 1,313–43.
6 Mark Mazower, *Dark continent: Europe's twentieth century* (London, 1998), 41.
7 T.K. Wilson, *Frontiers of violence: conflict and identity in Ulster and Upper Silesia, 1918–1922* (Oxford, 2010).
8 See Robert John Lynch, *The partition of Ireland 1918–1925* (Cambridge, 2019), Ch. 7.
9 Patrick Buckland (ed.), *Irish unionism 1885–1923: a documentary history* (Belfast, 1973), 411.
10 R.F. Foster, *Vivid faces: the revolutionary generation in Ireland, 1890–1923* (London, 2015), 324.
11 Robert Lansing, *The peace negotiations: a personal narrative* (Boston, 1921), 97.
12 Bill Kissane, *The politics of the Irish Civil War* (Oxford, 2005), 50.
13 Ibid., 53.
14 Éamon de Valera, *Ireland's request to the government of the United States of America for recognition as a sovereign independent state* (Washington D.C., 1920), 6, 7, 15; John Bowman, *De Valera and the Ulster question 1917–1973* (Oxford, 1989), 38.
15 David Fitzpatrick, *Descendancy: Irish Protestant histories since 1795* (Cambridge, 2014), Ch. 6 (quotation on 132).
16 Daniel Jackson, *Popular opposition to Irish Home Rule in Edwardian Britain* (Liverpool, 2009).

[17] Thomas Sinclair, 'The position of Ulster', in S. Rosenbaum (ed.), *Against Home Rule: the case for the union* (London, 1912), 172.

[18] *Irish Independent*, 23 Aug. 1918.

[19] *Belfast News Letter*, 17 Oct. 1921.

[20] Buckland, *Irish unionism*, 416.

[21] Marc Mulholland, 'Why did unionists discriminate?', in Sabine Wichert (ed.), *From the United Irishmen to twentieth-century unionism: essays in honour of A.T.Q. Stewart* (Dublin, 2004), 204.

[22] Richard Hawkins, 'Bates, Sir (Richard) Dawson', *Dictionary of Irish Biography*, https://www.dib.ie/biography/bates-sir-richard-dawson-a0491 (accessed 25 Nov. 2021).

[23] Bowman, *De Valera and the Ulster question*, 44.

[24] Richard Murphy, 'Walter Long and the making of the Government of Ireland Act, 1919–20', *Irish Historical Studies*, vol. 25, no. 97 (1986), 84.

[25] David Fitzpatrick, 'Historians and the commemoration of Irish conflicts, 1912–23', in John Horne and Edward Madigan (eds), *Towards commemoration: Ireland in war and revolution 1912–1923* (Dublin, 2013), 127, 129.

THE IRISH PROBLEM

The Irish Problem. (With apologies to Alice.), *The Westminster Gazette* (25 July 1921).

PRONI, D1415/A/11

PRONI, INF/7/B/3/28

Fintona horse tram on last night of service (30 Sep. 1957), *Belfast News Letter*.

Index

NOTE: Entries in italics relate to illustrations.

The Short SC.1 VTOL research aircraft making a vertical landing on a football pitch at Belfast during flight trials (7 Nov. 1958).

PRONI, D2334/1/5/10

Construction of the Silent Valley reservoir (1931).

PRONI, WAT/1/3/G/1/11

The Planetarium, Armagh (Sep. 1967).
PRONI, INF/7/A/16/87

Lough Shore Road, Portaferry, County Down (Nov. 2021).

Ulster Historical Foundation is pleased to acknowledge financial support
for this publication received from the Northern Ireland Office.
The Foundation would also like to thank the Centenary Historical
Advisory Panel for their support and input during the course of the project.

DUSTJACKET CAPTIONS
1 'The Shadow' (1957) by E. Rutherford. THE POLICE MUSEUM, BELFAST AND THE ARTIST'S FAMILY;
2 John Hewitt, poet. DERMOTT DUNBAR; 3 Ruby Murray, singer and actor. BELFAST TELEGRAPH;
4 Ashton Street Playscheme (Belfast), 1976. BELUM.W2015.118.1.29 (NMNI) © PHILIP WOODS;
5 De Lorean car, Belfast. BELFAST TELEGRAPH; 6 Lord Diljit Rana, entrepreneur and community
representative. ROGER HARRIS (https://members.parliament.uk/member/3689/portrait); 7 Jonathan
Bardon, historian and educator. CAROL TWEEDALE BARDON; 8 *Glór Uladh 1893–1943*. RUAIRÍ Ó
BLÉINE; 9 Helen Lewis, choreographer and dance teacher. PACEMAKER PRESS; 10 Prof. Dame Jocelyn
Bell Burnell, astrophysicist. UNIVERSITY OF DUNDEE; 11 SDLP election poster. PRONI, D4629/1/6/1;
12 DUP election poster. PRONI, D230/14/10/1; 13 Foyle Pride, Derry. BRENDAN HARKIN; 14 Joe Devlin,
politician and Nationalist Party leader. NPA PERS57, NATIONAL LIBRARY OF IRELAND; 15 Lady Mary
Peters LG, athlete and philanthropist. AARON McCRACKEN; 16 Stormont in the course of
construction. PRONI, D1415/D/14; 17 Basil Brooke, longest serving Prime Minister of Northern
Ireland (1943–63). PRONI, INF/7/5/250; 18 Anna Lo, politician and community representative. KEVIN
COOPER; 19 Bishop's Gate, Derry, 1920. THE ILLUSTRATED LONDON NEWS; 20 Sheelagh Murnaghan,
barrister and politician. *Sheelagh Murnaghan, 1924–1993: Stormont's only Liberal MP* (2019);
21 Milk Marketing Board logo. PRONI, AG/15/94; 22 Ruefrex, punk band (1983). ALASTAIR GRAHAM.

NOTE: the images used in the dustjacket design are merely intended to reflect
different aspects of life in Northern Ireland.

The Foundation would like to thank the following organisations and individuals for assistance
provided and for permission to reproduce images in the book. ORGANISATIONS: Alamy Stock Photo
(and individual contributors); Arts Council of Northern Ireland; *Belfast News Letter*; *Belfast
Telegraph*; Cork City and County Archives Service; Getty Images (and individual contributors);
The Illustrated London News; *Irish Independent*; David Lennon Art; Macmillan Publishers
International Limited; Magee College Community Collection, Ulster University Library; Martin
Nangle, the Director of the National Archives of Ireland; National Gallery of Ireland; National
Library of Ireland; National Museums NI (NMNI); Pacemaker Press; The Police Museum, Belfast;
The David Rumsey Map Collection, David Rumsey Map Center, Stanford Libraries;
studiohelen.co.uk; University of Dundee; *The Westminster Gazette*; and the Deputy Keeper
of the Records, the Public Record Office of Northern Ireland (PRONI).

INDIVIDUALS: Carol Tweedale Bardon, Keith Beattie, Alice Berger-Hammerschlag, Sophia
Campbell, Emma Connolly, Kevin Cooper, Dermott Dunbar, Yvonne Friers, Alastair Graham,
Carol Graham, Brendan Harkin, Roger Harris, David Holmes, Peter Leary, the Lewis family,
Declan Martin, Clement McAleer, Leanne McCormick, Aaron McCracken, Iain McCready,
Sammy McKay, Gordon McMullan, Ruairí Ó Bléine, Sean O'Neill (Spit Records), the Rutherford
family, Margaret Scull, Doug Sobey, the Turtle family, Philip Woods and Donovan Wylie.
We apologise in advance for any omissions or errors and will seek to rectify such
oversights in any future edition of this work.

Published 2022 by Ulster Historical Foundation
www.ancestryireland.com

ISBN 978-1-913993-16-0
Design by Dunbar Design
Printed by Gráficas Castuera